ROUTLEDGE LIBRARY EDITIONS: CURRICULUM

Volume 12

GUIDANCE AND THE CHANGING CURRICULUM

GUIDANCE AND THE CHANGING CURRICULUM

W. P. GOTHARD AND E. GOODHEW

LONDON AND NEW YORK

First published in 1987 by Croom Helm

This edition first published in 2019
by Routledge
2 Park Square, Milton Park, Abingdon, Oxon OX14 4RN

and by Routledge
711 Third Avenue, New York, NY 10017

Routledge is an imprint of the Taylor & Francis Group, an informa business

© 1987 W. P. Gothard and E. Goodhew

All rights reserved. No part of this book may be reprinted or reproduced or utilised in any form or by any electronic, mechanical, or other means, now known or hereafter invented, including photocopying and recording, or in any information storage or retrieval system, without permission in writing from the publishers.

Trademark notice: Product or corporate names may be trademarks or registered trademarks, and are used only for identification and explanation without intent to infringe.

British Library Cataloguing in Publication Data
A catalogue record for this book is available from the British Library

ISBN: 978-1-138-31956-1 (Set)
ISBN: 978-0-429-45387-8 (Set) (ebk)
ISBN: 978-1-138-31854-0 (Volume 12) (hbk)
ISBN: 978-1-138-32165-6 (Volume 12) (pbk)
ISBN: 978-0-429-45450-9 (Volume 12) (ebk)

Publisher's Note
The publisher has gone to great lengths to ensure the quality of this reprint but points out that some imperfections in the original copies may be apparent.

Disclaimer
The publisher has made every effort to trace copyright holders and would welcome correspondence from those they have been unable to trace.

GUIDANCE AND THE CHANGING CURRICULUM

W.P. GOTHARD and E. GOODHEW

CROOM HELM
London • New York • Sydney

© 1987 W.P. Gothard and E. Goodhew
Croom Helm Ltd, Provident House, Burrell Row,
Beckenham, Kent, BR3 1AT
Croom Helm Australia, 44-50 Waterloo Road,
North Ryde, 2113, New South Wales

Published in the USA by
Croom Helm
in association with Methuen, Inc.
29 West 35th Street,
New York, NY 10001

British Library Cataloguing in Publication Data

Gothard, W.P.
1. Education — Great Britain —
Curricula
I. Title II. Goodhew, E.
375'.00941   LB1564.G7
ISBN 0-7099-3825-X

Library of Congress Cataloging in Publication Data
ISBN 0-7099-3825-X

Word processing and layout by
B. Hargreaves (Audio Visual), Northampton
Printed and bound in Great Britain by
Biddles Ltd, Guildford and King's Lynn

CONTENTS

INTRODUCTION	1
CHAPTER 1 SCHOOLS, GUIDANCE AND VOCATIONALISM	2
CHAPTER 2 THE DEVELOPMENT OF THE PASTORAL CURRICULUM AND THE NEW ROLE OF THE TUTOR	12
CHAPTER 3 VOCATIONAL EDUCATION AND LIFE AFTER SCHOOL	47
CHAPTER 4 CAREERS EDUCATION UNDER PRESSURE	85
CHAPTER 5 POLITICAL EDUCATION - TOO HOT TO HANDLE?	109
CHAPTER 6 MANAGING CHANGE: TWO CASE STUDIES	128
CHAPTER 7 A NEW CURRICULUM?	142
APPENDICES	152
REFERENCES AND FURTHER READING	155
INDEX	165

INTRODUCTION

The great debate, begun by Prime Minister Callaghan at Ruskin College in October 1976, continues and this book is both a contribution to and an analysis of that debate. In 1979, the derisive Conservative election slogan "Educashun is'nt working" made it clear that the Thatcher government was intent on "making it work". It is now much more apparant to what ends this is directed, with "wealth creation" and "national cohesion" becoming the Government's main aims for education. Achieving these aims has proved difficult and has meant new means of central intervention. In this respect, the Manpower Services Commission has proved to be an ideal tool. Schools have come under close scrutiny and subject to interventions like TVEI. This has meant the powerful humanistic traditions in schooling have been under challenge, leading to any tensions. By exploring these tensions, it makes it possible to assess the likely direction of schooling.

CHAPTER 1

SCHOOLS, GUIDANCE AND VOCATIONALISM

> "We might take as our principal aim for secondary education the promotion of dignity. This was earlier defined as a sense of being worthy, of possessing creative, inventive and critical capacities, of having the power to achieve personal and social change". Hargreaves, (1982).

The aims and concerns of schooling are many and varied. For instance, Silver (1983) identifies ten issues that have been at the forefront of education since 1944 and of these, one in particular demands special attention. Silver describes this issue as the "Social functions of education", "which range through questions of the social and welfare aspects of education to the curative and socially useful functions of schools with regard to salient social problems. Debates about these issues raised questions of the relationships between educational institutions and the wider society and increasingly between schools and higher education on the one hand, and industry and employment (or unemployment) on the other hand". It will be argued that this, more than any other issue, most accurately describes the crucial changes that are taking place in our schools.

Eggleston (1977) perceives schooling as a "large and complex pattern of interactions" which overlap and interlock with each other. These interactions form a system made up of the curriculum, examinations, teaching, control and administration. At the heart of this system are a set of values and power relations, which are linked to the wider values and power relations of the society and the economy, as a whole. Thus, according to Eggleston, "the curriculum is one of the key areas in which the values and power system of the school and society areas come together; a key mechanism of social control over the young and over those who teach them". He goes on to define the curriculum as "the presentation of knowledge and learning experiences in the school".

Any curriculum is arrived at by a process of selection which will involve in Eggleston's words, five key factors.
(1) the definition of what shall be regarded as knowledge, understanding, values and skills,
(2) the evaluation of this knowledge - into areas of greater or lesser importance and status.
(3) the principles on which such knowledge shall be distributed; to whom and at what time various kinds of knowledge shall be made available and from whom it shall be withheld.
(4) the identity of the groups whose definitions prevail in these matters.
(5) the legitimacy of those groups to act in these ways.

Different purposes but the same direction?

If we look more closely at the nature of schooling, it is possible to discern two broad and apparently different activities. On the one hand, there is the traditional concern for teaching, based upon a formal curriculum that is taught to groups of pupils, and for most pupils, at 16 is assessed. On the other hand, there is a concern and caring for the individual pupil, based upon the pupil's personal circumstances and especially focussing on problems and crises in their life. The latter activity has always been present within schools, but in recent years has become more organised, professionalised and diversified. It has emerged under various titles such as "pastoral care, guidance and counselling", and certain job titles have become common like tutor, year head, house head, etc. As a result, schools have developed a parallel organisational structure (Best et al, 1980) based on the one hand upon academic departments or faculties and on the other on various pastoral systems such as year groups, houses etc. Whilst this change in structure symbolises the present apparently "schizophrenic" character of schooling, it is possible to see a convergence of activities within a growing "pastoral curriculum", which in the words of the White Paper, "Better Schools", DES 1985, is being "fostered systematically", within schools.

Alongside this development, there have been much

3

publicised developments in vocational education, particularly through the Technical and Vocational Education Initiative (TVEI) funded by the Manpower Services Commission (MSC). The intention behind such changes is quite clear-cut, and are stated in the White Paper "Better Schools" (DES 1985); "TVEI embodies the Government policy that education should better equip young people for working life". Since the great debate in 1977, the concept of vocational relevance has taken on greater significance within curriculum priorities, so that "Better Schools" (DES 1985) makes the point that "all the elements of a broad 5-16 curriculum are vocational in the sense that they encourage qualities, attitudes, knowledge, understanding, comprehensions which are necessary for employment". Bates et al (1984) however are under no illusions as to the present direction of schooling. They note "the rise of 'work in the curriculum' - leading to a fundamental reorientation of the school curriculum, especially as it affects the working class, from a liberal humanist and relatively autonomous perspective, to a much more technicist-applied and industry-linked perspective".

Silver (1983) identifies this as a long running debate between the liberal and the vocation in twentieth century British Education. In the 1980s he sees "under the impact of economic recession, structural unemployment, international competition and an acute awareness of major unresolved economic and social problems, pressures for vocational interpretations become more vigorous". The White Paper goes on to describe essential curriculum elements in the following terms "some awareness of economic matters, notably the operation of market forces, the factors governing the creation of private and public wealth, and tax, is a prerequisite for citizenship and employment, and health and sex education, taught within a moral framework, are a necessary preparation for responsible adulthood". Encapsulated within this policy statement, there lies the two broad developments which form the basis of this book, the "new vocationalism" and the pastoral curriculum. Immediately underlying such developments, is an ideological debate that requires close examination. Bates et al (1984) state the position clearly in saying "currently we can see a clear battle over whether the school should produce an 'ideal worker' to help resolve the economic crises or a 'critical and independent' person who can develop their own capabilities to the full. As we shall see, this is often apparently resolved by the former

pretending to be the latter".
"Better Schools" (DES 1985) firmly makes the point that "the government's principal aims for all sectors of education are first, to raise standards at all levels of ability and second, since education is an investment in the nation's future, to receive the best possible return from resources which are found for it". Quite clearly, a very functional "accounting" approach is being presented which is developed in greater detail in the White Paper as a whole. However, these two principal aims can be seen as directly linked to some of the major themes outlined in the Green Paper "Education in Schools" (DES 1977) that followed Callaghan's much publicised Ruskin speech the previous year. Moore (1984) describes the Green Paper's real theme as "teaching about the world of work and this is something much broader than teaching for it. It is a way of teaching about (and for) the social order, of promoting a particular vision of 'our society'". He goes on to state that "the essence of the paper's vision is a society without inner conflicts and divisions. The aspects of social change denoted by phrases 'technological change', multiracial, multicultural, the disappearance of the old stereotypes of the sexes' rather than with the frustrations, tensions and conflicts they actually entail".

The attack on "progressivism"

The Green Paper of 1977 and the White Paper that followed eight years later, although emanating from two different governments, do chart a steady, clearly defined trend, described by Sarup (1982) as "the attack on progressivism, the enforcement of stricter discipline, the emphasis on work socialisation and the increasing concentration of power". Progressivism has been a major movement within education that stems back to Dewey (1916) and focusses on the child centred approach. It maintains that education should concentrate on individual development with a minimum of imposition from above.
Hughes (1971) writes that "phrases associated with the child centred movement have now become familiar.... the whole child, creative self expression, teaching children not subjects, adjusting the school to the child, real-life experiences, teacher-pupil relationships, the needs of the learner, the importance of individual differences, personality development, intrinsic motivations, bridging the gap between school and the home....".

Schools, Guidance and Vocationalism

The phrases contrast strongly with the principal aims of "Better Schools" and herald a "new realism" in official educational thinking. The White Paper does occasionally pay "lip service" to progressivism in statements like "pupils need more opportunity to learn for themselves, to express their own views and to develop their ideas through discussion; teachers do too much for them". However, the predominant theme is clear: "more rapid technological change in an increasingly competitive world places a premium on enterprise, personal versatility and rational criticism. These values are the goal, both of the government policy for education and of its policies for revitalizing the economy and for maintaining that freedom under the law which is the precondition of each individual's fulfilment".

Put in other terms, the White Paper is pointing to the fact that the structure of British capitalism is under threat by the twin forces of the new "technologies" and tough foreign competition. Clarke and Willis (1984) describe this predicament graphically when they write "There is no room for reluctant heroes in the sinking ship of HMS UK plc. In a word, this view wishes to subjugate young people more completely than ever before to the needs of industry and therefore to the needs of capital. Youth can only be helped by their own contribution towards making a more successful economy and along with it more jobs. The implications for careers teaching and for work on the curriculum are obvious. The needs of industry, their 'sympathetic' presentation and production of 'model workers' threaten to carry all before them".

Although central, these pressing economic factors are not alone in determining the direction in which education is being propelled. There are a host of other social factors which have made an impact on schooling. To some extent these centre around social "problems" such as drug-taking, alcoholism, family breakdown, and promiscuity. Schools are required to respond to these issues and are put in the forefront of "dealing" with such problems, as well as being blamed by some politicians for allowing such problems to occur. At the same time, it is possible to discern an increasing radicalism amongst some teachers, particularly within London, which is expressed through ideologies such as feminism and anti-racism. Although they are a minority of the teaching profession, such teachers act as "ginger groups" for broader change.

Schools, Guidance and Vocationalism

Ideology and current issues

At this stage, it is useful to examine the role of ideology in relation to education. An ideology is a set or system of ideas that help individuals make sense of their relationship to the rest of society. As such, education is ultimately concerned with ideologies. Baron et al (1981) state that "ideas are properly called ideological when they can be shown to conceal or to resolve in an idealistic or imaginary way the problematic character of social life. In the process of presenting a particular social order as harmonious, natural or in need of rescue from subversion or decay, ideological accounts serve also to secure the position of dominant social groups".

Smith (1973) suggests a typology of goals in ideologies in education which is helpful in understanding change within the education system. This typology outlines eight criteria which explain the way in which change does or does not take place, thus for example, it is possible to examine how far education develops or frustrates the individual's talents and personality. There are three concepts that have never been far from the centre of educational discussion and debate. These have emerged as crucial in recent years and form an important part of Smith's typology. Firstly, a number of factors have made the concept of equality crucial in post war educational circles. Education has been seen as a vehicle for equalising life chances and although this has come in for widely varying attacks from Right and Left, this is still a powerful concept. More recently the search for equality within education has been particularly directed to two especially disadvantaged groups, girls and blacks.

Secondly, the concept of relevance within the curriculum has been promoted in numerous educational reports. This is repeated in the White Paper "Better Schools" (1985) where it is described as one of four fundamental principles; the point is made that "all subjects should be taught in such a way as to make plain their link with the pupil's own experience and to bring out their applications and continuing value in adult life". It is possible to see curriculum relevance in two different senses. There is vocational education, as embodied in TVEI, which clearly designed to prepare young people for technical and commercial occupations. On the other hand, there is personal, social and careers education that is ; concerned with "life skills", moral and sexual issues, political questions and a host of other matters to do with the "adult" world rather than solely employment.

The third concept is personal growth and development. The HMI survey, Aspects of Education in England (1979) mentions "the personal and social development of the pupil as one way of describing the central purpose of education". However, the concept can be seen as so broad as to be of little value, and consequently requires some clarification. David (1983) offers a wide range of definitions from various sources. For example, it can be understood as growth towards maturity and responsible citizenship. There is a good deal of agreement that personal and social education is engaged in the areas of values, decision making and personal relationships. Typically, it goes "beyond the didactic to embrace problem solving situations, decision making exercises, group discussion, simulation and games".

The Pastoral care system in a school has become the "vehicle" for delivering much of this, and the need for these systems has become accepted at all levels in education. However, how pastoral care operates in practice and in whose interests is open to debate. For instance, Sarup (1982) observes that "pastoral care in schools is based on a ´personal knowledge´ of pupils and help is given to deal with their problems. But at some stage, other agencies are called in. What may appear as a compassionate concern for the individual child is really an attempt to socialize the ´deviant´. Pastoral care thus becomes an inculcation of the ´expressive order´..... with the increasing intervention of the State, there is a growth in the ideology of pastoral care, involving teachers, social workers, police and doctors in this problem, the problem of youth ´discipline´ and ´order´". The growth of pastoral care and the increasing emphasis on personal growth and development in schools is closely linked to the guidance and counselling movement, (Hughes 1985) and it is importance to consider the impact of this movement upon secondary education as a whole.

The Guidance and Counselling Movement

Hughes (1971) describes guidance as being "identified by a tradition of help and service to individual children, involving not only care for rights but also for needs". He sees the slow struggle for social justice and a changing economy as two major factors contributing to the growth of guidance within schools. Freedom and self determination are the

Schools, Guidance and Vocationalism

recurring themes in guidance literature which firmly weds the concept to the Western (especially the American) democratic tradition (Bolger 1982). Beck (1971) in a wide survey of American guidance literature describes the most common traits "deemed desirable in a democracy" as productive, healthy, self-governing co-operative, socially efficient, ethically sensitive. At first sign, those traits arouse little discussion but on further examination, it is essential to ask such questions as who defines socially efficient, what is productive and what is not, and finally co-operative to what ends? Such terms only have meaning within a social context; a context that can be either fundamentally conflict-ridden or basically unified and stable depending on the particular perspective that is applied.

Guidance, whilst being concerned with helping, caring and self determination, can also be concerned with "cooling out" those who are unsuccessful in the exam system or who do not get employment. It can be a system as much concerned with the frustration of the individual as with individual growth. Much of the earlier optimism underlying the concept of guidance seems misplaced and perhaps naive in a society increasingly wracked by unemployment, discrimination, erosion of public services, public disorder, and other social forces. However, the underlying principles applying to the guidance and counselling movement still represent a positive and hopeful element for far reaching change within schools.

Shertzer and Stone (1981) identify six basic principles of guidance.
(1) Guidance is concerned primarily and systematically with the personal development of the individual.
(2) The primary mode by which guidance is conducted lies in individual behavioural processes.
(3) Guidance is oriented towards co-operation, not compulsion.
(4) Humans have the capacity for self development.
(5) Guidance is based upon recognising the dignity and worth of individuals as well as their right to choose.
(6) Guidance is a continuous, sequential, educative process.

Clearly, this conception of guidance is very much concerned with valuing each individual and creating opportunities for each pupil to learn about him/herself in a planned way over a period of time. This form of guidance can only work effectively if the school is committed to these principles and appoint staff who are appropriately trained and who have the resources to carry out this demanding role. There are signs that this is happening (Hughes 1985), but there is always a tension between a pupil centred guidance programme and other areas of school life, life within the local community and society as a whole where there is a very different emphasis upon the importance of the pupil's needs.

Counselling and guidance has not been accepted in schools without critical comment. Richardson (1979) discusses a number of objections to personal counselling in schools. He points out that pupils run the risk of being labelled, as a result of counselling. However, labelling unfortunately occurs without counselling taking place, and a good counsellor should seek to dispel these labels. Richardson feels that counselling individualises problems, which may deflect attention away from deficiences within the institution, whilst it may also be seen as an intrusion into pupils' private lives. Both points are well made. Counsellors should be seeking to help change their institutions as well as their clients, although the former is likely to prove a more formidable task than the latter. Similarly, a skilled counsellor will be aware of the danger of being intrusive and will be most careful to protect the confidentiality of their clients.

In recent years, the concept of guidance has been closely linked to vocational preparation (Miller 1983). The Further Education Unit (FEU) has been instrumental in these developments and in one of their documents (1981), an aim of vocational preparation is described as "to encourage them to become progressively responsible for their own development". Miller suggests that guidance can assist tutors in making this aim a reality. A five fold model of guidance is proposed that includes taking action, advising, teaching, informing and counselling, with the "underlying aims of guidance to help the student more towards self reliance rather than make the student dependent on tutor". There is a clear message in this model that the tutor needs to move away from advice to a more flexible, student centred approach. Indeed, Miller describes the aims of vocational preparation and of guidance as highly congruent with one another.

It is when Miller enters the discussion of values that his commitment to counselling becomes apparent. He suggests that tutors need to subscribe to values of openness, equality of worth and trust in order to provide a readiness to learn in a self directed way on the student. Miller identifies the qualities of acceptance, respect, empathy, and genuiness as conditions for an effective relationship between the tutor and the student. Whilst this can be seen as an important step in making vocational preparation more student centred, some caution has to be expressed. Statements need to be converted into practice and staff training is essential in this process. Similarly, there has to be an institutional as well as a personal commitment to the aims and values of counselling, otherwise mixed messages will be conveyed to students. Ultimately, the question of a conflict of interests arise when the needs of the individual student are considered in relation to the demands of the institution, whether this is a technical college, a managing agent or an employer.

If we return to the quotation from Hargreaves at the beginning of this chapter, we see how much guidance and counselling lies at the heart of his principal aim for secondary education, the "promotion of dignity". However, this is exceedingly difficult to achieve for pupils subjected to sexism and racism, the threat of unemployment or labelled as "misfits" and dropouts by the school system. The "sense of being worthy" is unlikely in a large impersonal institution severely stretched through lack of resources, and attacked on all sides as being ineffective. Developing each pupil's "creative, inventive and critical capacities" becomes possible in an educational setting with plenty of well trained, committed and well paid teachers, but this has become less and less possible with the policies of the Thatcher government. Finally, "the power to achieve personal and social change" does lie within our schools, but it is only possible if it comes to fruition within a society that is willing to foster and accept this change. A well organised, and properly resourced guidance and counselling programme can act as a "catalyst" within a school to help bring about these aims. During the sixties and early seventies, it seemed that this was happening, albeit slowly, but the last ten years have witnessed a retrenchment in this trend. The reasons for these changes will be explored in subsequent chapters.

CHAPTER 2

THE DEVELOPMENT OF THE PASTORAL CURRICULUM AND THE NEW ROLE OF THE TUTOR

> "The Art of the Pastoral System is to help all individuals without always giving individual help" - Michael Marland (1980).

Marland's statement, in justification of the need for what he called a "pastoral curriculum" indicated a change which was taking place in the perception of the place of the pastoral system within the school. Pastoral systems had often been regarded as necessary for administration, discipline, and crisis response rather than for the systematic planning of the welfare of all individuals. Marland argued, however, that:-

> "a school must find ways of preparing for the expected needs, following up the discovered needs, and giving the necessary basis for a personal seeking of advice".

He went on to argue that:-

> "the most effective individual guidance and counselling depends on the background of concepts, facts, and skills which the individual client brings to the counselling session. I would therefore suggest that individual counselling has to depend on whole group exploration of this necessary background".

Drawing up the list of what should go into that background, is, he said, essentially a curriculum matter.

> "The curriculum components which relate especially to individual and personal

The Pastoral Curriculum

growth I would call the 'pastoral curriculum'".

Background to Pastoral Care

Marland had already argued earlier that the school's pastoral undertaking was "the central one" (1974). The pastoral focus was, he argued, wider than mere learning and "as I see it," he said, "the school is its pastoral organisation". This made necessary the setting up of pastoral systems because it was, he argued, "a truism of school planning that what you want to happen must be institutionalized".

It would be wrong, however, to assume that teachers are in agreement as to what the term "pastoral care" means. A "brainstorm" of teachers might throw up words and phrases like:- "welfare", "personal development", "monitoring progress", "coping skills", "decline of the extended family", "larger schools", "whole school policies", "preventative", "problem-solving", "vocational", "divorce", "violence", "unemployment", "discipline", "counselling", "administration" and others such as "bandwagon" and "empire-building". (Goodhew 1981). Research in a large comprehensive school has indicated that although staff felt pastoral care to be important they did not regard it as "having a central educative purpose in itself". (Marland 1974). Staff in the school felt that pastoral care systems should be supportive of both pupils and staff and that there should be clearly defined procedures for an emergency. One teacher felt that the purpose of pastoral care was to look after the child's welfare throughout the school. As a tutor, you should "have an overview of the child - whatever problem somebody in your tutor group gets into then it is your responsibility - you have to do your best to iron it out". Another teacher commented that "as pastoral care systems work out they are largely administrative systems", while another said that "too often the pastoral system is very much a disciplinary organisation, making life unpleasant for a small number of pupils". One view was that pastoral care "should back up the academic and extra curricular activities of the school, to help the child if it has problems and then just keep out of the way...." This teacher went on to castigate pastoral staff for "....in many cases abrogating the responsibility of parents". The same teacher felt that pastoral care was "a system which has grown with comprehensive schools and is now largely out of control.... because

13

it is there people are now trying to justify it and find uses for it".

This research showed that the Head of Year was expected to act as some kind of disciplinary figure, allowing the tutor to be a more "pastoral" person. As one member of staff put it "I see the tutor more involved, and the Head of Year a bit removed because he cannot afford to become too friendly.... ....you tend to wave the Head of Year in front of them and say ′right, if you carry on like this you will go straight to Mr. -----′". Perhaps typical of many of the comments was "My most important task is looking after the welfare of the individual kid in my class.... any trouble, any problems.... dealing with things as they are.... <u>muddling through actually</u> .... sorting things out on a one to one level". (my italics). As for training for pastoral care, one said his training was "a quick crash course when I started teaching on how to mark the register.... since I have been teaching its a case of picking things up as you go along". One member of staff did not want too much intervention from pastoral staff:- "the main difficulty I find is the stuff that comes down from the pastoral staff: very often you are dealing out study schemes.... you do so much clerical and administrative work that to actually sit down and talk to an individual for a quarter of an hour, to get to know them, I find very difficult, because you keep getting these interruptions". In answer to a questionnaire 96% of staff felt that "to get to know pupils in the tutor group" was important or very important (compared with only 32% of pupils) but as one member of staff admitted: "it is difficult to get to know individuals.... The danger is that you get to know a few very well - those who are willing to help you out - the quieter ones you don′t really get to know".

It is clear, therefore, that staff in this school did not see pastoral care in terms of curriculum input. The concerns were that each pupil should be well known to a member of staff, that administration should be possible and that there should be a strong disciplinary system in which pastoral staff are seen to be backing up the subject teachers. There was also an awareness of the dialectic between "care" and "control". The concept of the role of the Year Head as being a disciplinary figure puts a great deal of responsibility on the Form Tutor as far as pastoral care is concerned. Yet tutors too have disciplinary functions in their day-to-day teaching and a number of those interviewed mentioned the problem of the

The Pastoral Curriculum

conflicting roles of "tutor" and "teacher", especially if they taught their own form. The Year Head, who often attempts to combine the disciplinary function with a "counselling" one, may have similar problems.

The views expressed by staff in the school where this piece of research took place would not seem to be unique. Best, Ribbins and Jarvis (1982) found similar views expressed in their researches at "Rivendell" School. They found that it was possible to distinguish between what they called the "conventional wisdom" of pastoral care and the actual experience of it in schools. In the conventional wisdom (as described by writers such as Marland and Blackburn) they say, pastoral care is viewed as an essential aspect of educational provision, facilitated by pastoral care structures, with "houses", year groups, counsellors, careers advisers, heads of year, form tutors, etc. These structures are seen to be support-giving, reassuring, convivial institutions whose functioning makes possible the fullest and happiest development of the individual pupil's school career. The growth of these structures is explained as a response on the part of those who organise and administer education to:- a growing awareness of the non-academic needs of children; the proliferation of choices and potential problems confronting children in large modern schools; the anxiety-prone nature of advanced urban-industrial societies and the rapid rate of social change; the increasing complexity of family and community life, coupled with the decline of the extended family and a rapidly growing divorce rate. Pastoral care was, therefore, seen as a "good thing" and unproblematic in itself.

The research of Best, Ribbins and Jarvis suggests, however, that there is a gulf between the theory and what actually happens. There appears, they say, to exist among teachers and others an "unofficial" version of pastoral care which stands in stark contrast to the "official" version. In this alternative version "pastoral care" is a nuisance, an impossible, impractical, and largely unnecessary, diversion from the "real" job of teaching. The structures appear to have more to do with providing the school with a workable division into teams for sports and other competitions than they have to do with genuine concern for the welfare of pupils. So-called "pastoral care" periods are actually provided to facilitate petty administrative functions, such as marking the register, reading school notices and so

The Pastoral Curriculum

on. It is, they say, unusual for these periods to be used in conscious attempts to "guide" or "counsel"; more frequently the time is used in idle chatter or administrative and disciplinary activities.

Hamblin (1978), too, emphasises that there are a number of distortions of the pastoral care system. "A visitor to a school, who had no knowledge of education might still suspect that the pastoral care system was malfunctioning. He might note that although the headmaster had given form tutors pastoral care periods, they were used by pupils to do homework whilst the teacher talked to individuals. He could go away with the idea that pastoral care consisted of a somewhat vague attempt to get to know the pupils and be unable to describe the techniques used". He argues that there is an ever greater need for such periods to be well organised and stimulating than for subject periods since they are concerned with personal development. "Sadly", he says, "there is a tendency to turn the pastoral system into a punishment system". In some schools, he says, the function of the pastoral care system is conceived largely in terms of complaints, investigation of those complaints and finally, of punishment. He argues that "this trend seems to encourage the weak teacher to abdicate the responsibility for maintaining control during teaching. If the pastoral team accept the punishment role, then the tendency will increase, and it will prevent the pastoral system from performing a positive function". "Perhaps", he says, "we tend to confuse punishment and discipline".

Best et al (1980) point out that with the increased size of schools, mixed ability teaching, the raising of the school leaving age and more public examinations the problems of administration and control are amplified. Recalcitrant pupils are now a feature of _all_ schools and _all_ classes or teaching groups: pastoral care may be a mechanism for the imposition of tighter discipline on them. As they put it "an empirical investigation may show ´pastoral care´ to be less concerned with the problems of pupil welfare than with the problem of social control and administrative convenience following substantial changes in the provision and organisation of secondary education". So, "pastoral care could be a deliberately evolved device for managing a potentially dangerous situation which enables the teacher to remain in control". It is often the feeling of pastoral practitioners that they are expected to make up for the inadequacies of the

The Pastoral Curriculum

school in other areas - particularly in curriculum design. Hargreaves 1982 has emphasised too, the importance of the hidden curriculum which, he says, exerts on many pupils, particularly but by no means exclusively from the working class, a destruction of their dignity which is so massive and pervasive that few subsequently recover from it. He suggests that most pupils accept school with varying degrees of resignation as their lot; there is very little they can do about it. "But there is a distinct minority which reacts with overt bitterness and hostility and the issue at stake is how we interpret that reaction". Hargreaves´ interpretation is that pupil opposition is an indication that the pupils are rejecting school because schooling destroys their dignity. In response, the pupils set up an <u>alternative</u> means of achieving dignity and status by turning the school´s dignity system upside down. Dignity and status are earned by active hostility to school and teachers and the teachers contribute to this alternative system, paradoxically, by trying to subvert it, for whenever a teacher seeks to undermine it, he provides the opposition with yet a further opportunity of achieving status in the alternative system. As Hargreaves puts it "the counter-culture requires and depends for its existence upon teachers´ attempts to eradicate it. As a solution to the dignity problem it is exceedingly clever, for the harder teachers try to make these pupils conform, the more the counter-culture thrives". All of this has relevance to staff with posts of pastoral responsibility as these are often the ones in the "firing line", expected to back up staff experiencing difficulties with such pupils and to support the pupils through the school system as best they can. This "patch them up and send them back to the firing line" approach is something which rings true for many teachers.

Hargreaves´s analysis suggests, therefore, that opposition to school cannot be accounted for by neat psychological or sociological explanations of defective personality or poor home background. It also suggests that "pastoral care" often has a function of trying to ensure that this situation can be controlled in schools. As Williamson (1980) suggests, support is given in two quite different ways; on the one hand there are the more recognised methods of supporting the able child through a system to which he quickly adjusts, and on the other, those activities which are aimed at resolving the problems posed to the system by the not inconsiderable numbers

17

of children who are unable to benefit from what he calls "product" teaching and who may rebel against its constraints. This distinction, he says, calls into question some widely held notions about the functions of pastoral care systems and those who operate them: "while some children are ´guided´, ´counselled´ and ´supported´ through a successful school career, others (the ´less able´, the ´disadvantaged´, etc.) are ´processed´ to accept a system in which they are destined to be failures". This processing Williamson calls "pastoralisation". By this process the pupils who experience difficulties in learning through the traditional methods of teaching are led to accept the hours of boredom which current practices of education may entail for them:

"With these pupils, normally identified as the ´less able´, the tutor frequently uses the relationship of mutual trust, knowingly or otherwise, to deflect legitimate grievance away from the inadequate types of learning experience offered within the school. It is this ´pastoralisation´ which makes possible, or is even a precondition of, the continued existence of what might be called ´product teaching´; i.e. if education is approached as the production of a standardised commodity, the raw materials (children) have somehow to be induced to stay on the conveyor belt and accept the practices of the assembly men (teachers) as legitimate. When children question the adequacy of the learning situations provided, the tutor is faced with the difficult task of finding answers which will, at least, avert an open rejection of the school and its practices. The type of explanation he gives for these inadequacies leads, initially, to a spirit of glum tolerance among the pupils. Of serious concern for the secondary school is the way in which, as the pupils progress through the school, this glum tolerance gives way to a variety of attitudes of resentment towards the school in particular and society in general". Pastoralisation has, therefore, the negative function of reducing the resentment felt at the lack of opportunity offered and at the limited learning experiences provided. As Williamson says, "support of learning situations is a positive function of pastoral care: its support for inadequate teaching methods is an immediate cause for concern".

Historical background

The writings of Best et al, Hargreaves and Williamson

suggest that there may well be a gulf between what practitioners of pastoral care say, or believe, they are doing and what is actually happening "at the chalkface". Rather than providing a "warm, accepting and stable environment in which each pupil can maximise his or her potential", as a typical school brochure may say, they may be simply facilitating administration and social control, knowingly or not. The urgent necessity for good order and discipline in schools may lead to attempts to deal with the symptoms without attempting to diagnose the fundamental causes. Any such diagnosis is likely to be threatening to staff, many of whom will consider it to be unnecessary anyway. Underlying all this is a lack of consensus as to what is meant by pastoral care and the status that it should be given and this can lead to a vagueness about aims and an inherent tension within its practice between caring and controlling.

A look at the underlying historical influences affecting pastoral care can help to place current concepts into context and give a clearer understanding of them. Little research has been done into the historical background of pastoral care but the analyses of Lang (1984) and Blackburn (1980) provide a useful framework. Lang traces the development of pastoral care back to the reforms in the public schools in the late eighteenth and early nineteenth centuries. These reforms, associated with reforming headmasters of whom Thomas Arnold is the best known, were designed to change the public schools from sordid and brutal institutions into more enlightened establishments in which academic learning was to be accompanied by training to become a Christian gentleman. As Arnold himself put it: "And what I have often said before I repeat now: what we must look for here is, first, religious and moral principles, second, gentlemanly conduct, third, intellectual ability". All this had clear implications for the development of that side of the public school that has influenced pastoral care for it indicated a concern which went beyond mere academic learning. In the latter half of the century a ´muscular Christianity´ was added, as games playing became an important part of the curriculum, and this too had carried over into many comprehensives, via the Grammar Schools. The idea of a tutorial programme also developed as is indicated by the evidence an Eton tutor gave to the Clarendon Commission (1864):-

"The problem of numbers has been partly solved by putting each boy under a tutor whose connection with him remains unbroken during his whole stay in the school and whose duty it is to bestow that attention on him and undertake that responsibility for him that cannot be expected of the class teacher".

Public schools provided, therefore, the example of schools taking responsibility for the personal and social development of the child as well as the academic. They did so by organising activities in "Houses" and by having a tutorial system. Parts of the curriculum, in particular Games, were geared towards helping this development to happen. The public schools were not alone in this concern, however, as the elementary schools, too, provide a link with the pastoral care of today in that socialisation was an important aim. Robert Raikes, when he started the Sunday School movement, was concerned to keep the urchins off the streets while Robert Lowe wrote later that "the lower classes ought to be educated and discharge the duties cast upon them. They should also be educated that they may appreciate and defer to a higher cultivation when they meet it, and the higher classes ought to be educated in a very different manner, in order that they may exhibit to the lower classes that higher education to which, if it were shown to them, they would bow down and defer".

This element of control has continued through to modern times, as Williamson suggested and as is also suggested by the writer of an internal discussion document for the Department of Education and Science. "There has to be selection", the official writes, "because we are beginning to create aspirations off society cannot match...... When young people drop off the education production line and cannot find work at all, or work which meets their abilities and expectations, then we are only creating frustration with perhaps disturbing social consequences...... if we have an educated and idle population we may possibly anticipate more serious social conflict. People must be educated once more to know their place". Those involved with pastoral care would, in this analysis, be expected to play their part in ensuring that this happens. The other strand which emerged in the reformed public schools and in the philanthropic efforts which led to the setting up of elementary schools was that of care. The plight of the poor and the welfare of the young did concern many as did the belief that the poor were poor because of their own feckless attitudes and that attempts to help them materially would encourage their idle irresponsibility.

The Pastoral Curriculum

These themes of care and control can be seen continuing through the relatively small secondary schools of the twentieth century to the setting up of the first comprehensive schools in the early 1950s. These new schools were large and the anxiety was that the welfare of the individual child would be lost among the mass of pupils as would the sense of belonging that smaller schools tended to instil. Increased size also brought extra demands in terms of administration and made it necessary to consider a structure to ensure discipline and good order. The twin concerns of care and control, together with the extra administration, became the responsibility of staff in the new pastoral systems which were set up, systems which usually copied the idea of "houses" as used by the public schools. Power was delegated to "mini-heads" and their tutors who tried to instil a sense of belonging to the "house", to ensure that each child was well known by someone among the staff, to ensure the welfare of each child, to maintain discipline and to maintain an efficient organisation. This led to a new development in that many schools set up two systems side by side - the pastoral, with its heads of house and tutors, and the academic, with its heads of departments (or faculties) and subject teachers. The fact that most of the "teachers" were also "tutors" ensured that the split was not total but the possible role conflict for the "caring" tutor who was also a subject teacher was a cause for concern.

Since the late 1960s there has been increasing trend to heal this so-called pastoral/academic split as pastoral staff have become more and more involved in the curriculum. A more sophisticated programme of Careers education became necessary as the development of option schemes and the raising of the school leaving age gave impetus to the need to advise pupils about the subjects they might choose to study as well as to help them make realistic decisions about study or work beyond the age of sixteen. This was clearly a curriculum matter, especially as the concept of careers education emerged, implying a syllabus, often involving tutors as well as specialist careers teachers. Increasing awareness that many of the problems that appeared in school were an expression of problems which lay beyond it, including the problem of the children who were quietly conforming yet achieving little, led to an increased emphasis on counselling, either through a trained counsellor or through the pastoral head and tutor.

Attention focussed on the one-to-one relationship

between the pastoral head/tutor and the pupils in their care. This one-to-one model did, however, cause problems. Tutors had very little or no training in counselling so the quality of the "care" varied as tutors had to rely on "common sense" and experience. It was also difficult to build the kind of trusting relationship needed for confidential counselling within a group of thirty tutees and there was always the problem of what to do with the other 29 while one is being counselled. Much good work was, and still is, done but little was considered in an anticipatory way; the usual approach was to wait until the child expressed a problem and then try to deal with it, by which time it might be too late. It also became apparent that many problems were partly caused because of lack of information. Marland (1980) cites the example of the third-year girl, having rows about being home late at night, who has turned to her head of year for advice:-
"before he can give advice, he has a good deal of information to give. He actually has to remind her of what it is like to be a parent; he probably has to remind her about parents´ legal responsibilities, that parents themselves aren´t allowed to go out and abandon children under a certain age at home and so on... (the) advice session has become an instruction lesson". The argument is that it is impossible to focus on individual help and guidance without considering the curriculum content that lies behind it, in this case the rights and obligations of the adolescent.

Marlands proposal was, therefore, that every school should create a pastoral curriculum to establish the concepts, attitudes, facts and skills which are necessary to the individual; the individual cliet would then bring these to the counselling session. There would never be sufficient time for all pupils in a school to have all the necessary guidance given individually. Unless we have an agreed background curriculum, he argued, we are depending on children having crises before we can offer them any help. To rely too heavily on pastoral care given individually is actually a let down for the majority of children. A school must find ways of preparing for the expected needs, following up the discovered needs and providing the necessary basis for the personal seeking of advice. There was to be a move from a crisis-centred approach to a more anticipatory and educational approach. The pastoral curriculum was necessary to help tutors to help their pupils. Marland suggested that the content of the pastoral

The Pastoral Curriculum

curriculum can usefully be gathered under three headings - personal; educational; and vocational. Under these headings might be included:-

(a) Personal
1. The self; temperament, personality, needs.
2. How to assess, understand and cope with physical and emotional well-being.
3. The individual in relation to family, neighbours, friends, growing up.
4. Getting on with people, skills and attitudes.
5. Rights and obligations as an adolescent.
6. Choice and Choosing.
7. Using the facilities and services which society offers.
8. The personal conventions of society.
9. Charity, understanding.
10. Recreation, hobbies, using time, opportunities.

(b) Educational
1. The school as an organisation.
2. Study skills.
3. Subject choice.
4. The examination system.
5. Examination entry: administrative arrangements.
6. Other educational agencies outside school.
7. Newspapers, museums, magazines, broadcasting.
8. The sharing of educational experience in the tutor group.
9. Help pupils make use of the feedback on their learning performance that the school gives them.

(c) Vocational
1. Self-awareness.
2. Opportunity awareness.
3. Decision-making.
4. Transition to life after school.

This list was not meant to be prescriptive; neither was it suggested that all the pastoral curriculum should be taught in tutorial time. The tutorial programme would take those parts of the pastoral curriculum which it had been agreed in the individual school should go to the tutors. Other parts would be distributed to subject departments.

Douglas Hamblin (1978) had already argued that a long-term plan for pastoral care could be built around the "critical incidents" in a comprehensive school for pupils aged 11-18. The aims would be:-

23

The Pastoral Curriculum

1. To isolate points at which pupils are likely to affiliate with the school or dissociate from it.
2. To provide both the skills and perceptions which allow pupils to deal with these incidents constructively.

Examples of such critical incidents are:-

1. Entry into Comprehensive School

At this stage an induction programme is needed which helps the pupils adjust to new teaching situations; to develop homework and study skills; to cope with the expansion of social relationships; to help them understand the pastoral care system.

2. Third Year Subject Choices

Here a guidance programme is needed, dealing with reasons for choice, cost of choices; the nature of subjects; parental involvement; other influences etc. David Hargreaves (1982) tells of how he followed a class round in a school which operated a most elaborate system of "setting and options". With considerable ingenuity two girls had manipulated the system so that they always went to the same classes together. So much for rational choice!

3. Fifth Year

Preparation for examinations; decision whether to leave or stay at school. Here a programme is needed which gives extended study skills; strategies for effective revision; methods of coping with anxiety and negative feelings.

4. Sixth Form

At the beginning an induction programme is needed to ensure an understanding of the new demands of the Sixth Form. Guidance sessions of a personal and vocational nature are needed throughout the Sixth Form and preparation for a higher education programme later on.

Hamblin argues that the distinction between pastoral and academic is unreal and that the pastoral team is concerned with the production of the morally educated person who has developed the skill of

The Pastoral Curriculum

standpoint-taking and of empathy, as well as intellectual competence. Moral development, he says, includes the ability to read signals sent out by others; to present ones own views clearly and yet listen to those of others; to be ready to help rather than exploit the vulnerable; and to be able to make a positive emotional response when necessary. In doing this we need to enhance self-respect:-
"the pastoral care system should never become a device for labelling pupils as inadequate, but should be a means of instituting constructive innovations, rather than propping up the status quo and inhibiting change".
Much of this work can be done, he says, by structuring a programme around the critical incidents mentioned. If these critical incidents are successfully dealt with then the adolescent will be able to make full use of the resources of the school within the limits of his ability, but if they are evaded the difficulties of adjustment will increase.

Hamblin's argument is supported by research done by John Bazalgette (1983). Asked to work with a group of bright, underachieving and disruptive 5th Form girls, Bazalgette came to realise that the root of the girls' difficulties lay in their initial experience of making the transition into the secondary school. Faced with the apparent chaos of a large secondary school they had become increasingly anxious and frightened and had formed themselves into a close group, providing support, security and reassurance. The chaos and those who represented it - teachers, "good" pupils, unknown adults etc. - were kept out behind their shared "boundary" and potential threats were kept under control either by exclusion or by domination when they came too near.

"A pattern of behaviour evolved by 11-12 year olds to cope with the anxiety of their life in the first year had now become ossified but still held the girls in its grip four years later when the issues they now faced were, in fact, very different. At a stage which required them to make their own choices.... their learned response to anxieties was to band together and to assume a united front. The images of the environment which they must now enter were populated with grossly exaggerated figures most of which were negative".

Thus, their home grown solution to problems in the first year in school prevented them from working out the real issues in the 5th Year. Bazalgette concludes from this that the girls had not been given a lead in how to take up the pupil role in the school. The tutor should, he feels, make a strong contribution in helping the pupil to make sense of what is happening.

Hamblin and Marland have done much to outline the organisation and content of the pastoral curriculum. Hamblin (1978) also suggested an approach to teaching that content but it was Leslie Button (1974) who emphasised the importance of the methodology. Button claims that "our personal satisfaction, growth and development is achieved mainly through the part we play in the lives of other people and they in ours. Group work is about helping people in their growth and development, in their social skills, in their personal resource, and in the kind of relationships they establish with other people. Social skills can be learnt only in contact with other people, and it is the purpose of group work to provide the individual with opportunities to relate to others in a supportive atmosphere, to try new approaches and to experiment in new roles". For Button it is the experience reaching young people which forms the basis of the programme, and experience arises out of the approach even more than out of the content. "In fact, in his work, the approach is an important part of the content", he says (1983). He also argues (1980) that:-

1. Many pastoral systems are more about CONTROL and CONFORMITY than they are about the growth of social competence, personal responsibility and maturity.

2. Most social education programmes in schools seem to be about offering young people INFORMATION; they do not have any real impact on young people at an AFFECTIVE level.

3. This one-to-one casework model, where tutors concentrate on dealing solely with pupils individually is inappropriate:-

    - it is <u>crisis-centred</u> as distinct from educative or developmental.

    - the tutor may develop excellent individual relationships, yet his group may be divided among themselves, unsupportive, even destructive, of one another.

Button argues that "<u>to create a caring community in the tutorial group should be the basic aim of the</u>

The Pastoral Curriculum

tutor".

Button therefore argues for a developmental programme going by a step-by-step approach from:-

1. a study of the situations in which the pupils find themselves   TO

2. an examination of their own attitudes and behaviour   TO

3. an exploration of their manner and skills in coping with other people - friends, other peers, the opposite sex, parents, siblings, strangers, adults, people in authority   TO

4. their deeper self feelings which influence every department of life so strongly.

The most effective and efficient way to achieve all this, he says, is through group work.

Button attempts to provide a curriculum framework for this in "Group Tutoring for the Form Teacher" (1 & 2, 1982/83). The themes which would be sustained throughout the whole five year programme would include the pupil's place in the school; the pastoral group as a small caring community; relationships, the self and social skills; communication and listening skills; school work and study skills; academic guidance and careers education; health and hygiene; and personal interests. Each will feature to a different degree in each year's programme and it is important that the treatment should be cyclical rather than circular, so that the topic is treated with growing sophistication year by year.

Button puts the emphasis, therefore, on two main factors: the method (i.e. group work) and the tutor. Since it is the tutor who sees the group more often than any other teacher, and who is designated by schools to have responsibility for the welfare of the pupil, it is the tutor who is expected to use "the method" to promote the personal and social development of the pupil. The tutor will feel less the overall provider than he may feel when teaching a subject; he is expected to be much more a third party, enabling the whole group to develop their capacity for helping one another. "To some degree", says Button, "the tutor will be making caring for one

27

another legitimate, but it is likely also that the young people will need some help in learning how to help one another. This means that the quality of the experience for the young people is strongly bound up with the style of leadership offered by the tutor". (1983).

For Button, therefore, the role of the tutor is vital. However, tutors need to be helped in meeting these demands, both in terms of training and in materials for use in tutor time. The Active Tutorial Work Project has made a significant effort to meet both these needs. The Active Tutorial Work Booklets (6 volumes 1979-83) were written, initially, as a local curriculum development project in response to the demand from teachers in Lancashire for materials and guidance in their role as form tutors. Jill Baldwin and Harry Wells - curiculum development officers at Burnley and Blackburn Curriculum Development Centres - worked with a number of teachers to produce materials which were tested in schools and evaluated by teachers. The materials were changed as appropriate, but the process seemed to be successful and so the materials were published. In a structured way, and greatly influenced by Button's work, they attempt to give teachers guidance in the teaching of life-skills and personal relationships; there is also a great emphasis on helping pupils to cope with the pressures met in school. The work, in fact, aims at aiding the academic work of the school. The published materials are not, however, meant to be prescriptive - they are materials (which can be photocopied, legally) to help the hard-pressed teacher to achieve the desired objectives. They are a resource. They do not have to be followed slavishly, but they do provide an invaluable aid.

It is difficult, however, to carry out this kind of work without any training. Training programmes are aimed at:-

(a) giving teachers the chance to have the experience themselves of being a member of a group of this kind.

(b) helping teachers thus to understand the basic concepts which underlie the work.

These training programmes, financed by the Health Education Council, were aimed initially to introduce teachers to the group work methods involved, and then to train teachers to train others. In this way, as L.E.A.s set up support groups, continued development

The Pastoral Curriculum

was made possible independent of the original project.

The Pastoral Curriculum

Marland, Hamblin, Button, Baldwin and Wells bring attention to three important questions which schools have to consider when drawing up their pastoral curricula:-

- what should the pastoral curriculum contain?
- who should teach it?
- how should it be taught?

The decisions which schools make on these issues will be made in the light of their own circumstances and they will be crucial to the success or otherwise of the pastoral curriculum.

1. Content

Hamblin (1978) and Marland (1980) have already been referred to as giving useful models for organising the pastoral curriculum. Watkins (1985) defines the pastoral curriculum as "the school's learning offer which has a deliberate focus on the learner's learnings about him/herself" and suggests the following areas for this curriculum:-

- bodily self
- sexual self
- social self
- vocational self
- moral/political self
- organisational self

Themes to be covered and schemes of work to address these themes could thus be devised, bearing these areas in mind. This is a useful model as it indicates the genuinely cross-curricular nature of the pastoral curriculum and also brings into focus some of the curriculum materials and projects which already exist under these headings. Over the years schools have been inundated with materials from national and locally based projects concerning social education, social studies, moral education, health education, careers education, political education, general studies and humanities. As Williams and Williams (1980) point out "a common feature to all (these projects) is their eagerness to accentuate their unique and distinctive contribution to

29

education and hence their claim for curriculum time". As a result of this these projects often appear to be in competition with each other for the available curriculum time. As Williams and Williams say, "It is galling to see such competition arise because it contributes to the general confusion which exists in relation to this particular area of the curriculum. It would in contrast be immeasurably helpful to teachers and schools if they would spell out instead what affinities they might have with other projects and how they contribute to a more broadly based and unified programme of personal education".

Williams and Williams looked at a number of national curriculum projects - the Schools Council projects concerned with Health Education, Social Education, Moral Education, Political Education and the Humanities Curriculum Project - and found them to have a number of similarities:-

1. VALUES - Each is concerned with personal and social values and helping young people to clarify the values and attitudes they hold.

2. DECISION-MAKING - Each is concerned with helping young people make choices and decisions related to their personal and social lives.

3. RELATIONSHIPS - Each is concerned with developing awareness of and sensitivity to personal and social relationships of different kinds and with developing appropriate skills.

4. METHODOLOGIES - Each stresses the need for teaching methods which go beyond the traditional and didactic to embrace problem-solving situations, decision-making exercises, group discussion, simulation and games, opportunities for self-direction as well as for co-operative projects with others.

5. ACROSS THE CURRICULUM - Elements of each of the areas are to be seen in the traditional subject areas and can, therefore, be regarded as cross-curriculum activities.

As they say, "Each is directly concerned with the development of personal autonomy and the development and use of methodologies most suitable to attaining this goal with young people".

Another useful perspective for examining these similarities, they point out, is provided by Wilson's

The Pastoral Curriculum

(1970) components of moral education. These include:-
1. The ability to reason and make rational judgements.
2. The concepts and principles involved in concern for people.
3. Factual knowledge.
4. Alertness and determination; the need to translate what is taught into action.

It is evident, therefore, that the various curriculum projects in the field of personal and social education have much in common and that curriculum planning in this area is facilitated by looking at this commonality and using it in developing a coherent and co-ordinated curriculum. The importance of developing this kind of curriculum was highlighted by the Schools Council Working Party on Social Education which reported in 1983, (David, 1983). As the working party put it:-

"The complexities of a changing society make it essential that schools attempt to develop all the inner resources of students, emotional as well as intellectual. This development cannot be achieved in an ad hoc manner, or by dependence on the ethos of the school alone. It requires constructive thinking and planning, and properly structured programmes. The personal needs of young people in schools are varied, and different forms of family and school support meet physical, social, mental and spiritual requirements with varying success. Failure by family and school to meet such personal needs can bring lack of success in school, social cost to the community and personal unhappiness.

The development of young people is complicated by varying public and private influences in their lives and by the fact that the speed of change in our society is accelerating and confusing our planning and purpose. The list of changes is familiar, including for example, the rapid expansion of knowledge, the growth of media influence, the lessening of family stability and traditional authority, and increasing uncertainties in the world of work.... unemployment for young people is a major problem. Consideration of multicultural relationships has become a more obvious and major task, and the needs and aspirations of minority groups have emphasised our national cultural diversity, with obvious implications for work in schools".

The Pastoral Curriculum

Hopson and Scally (1981) also stress the importance of this area, using a needs analysis approach to define life skills. They suggest that someone leaving school today in the U.K. can expect:-

(a) three or four different occupations in his or her lifetime;
(b) six to ten changes of job;
(c) to move away from the area of the country in which they were born;
(d) probably have two marriages;
(e) to be involved in education at different points throughout their lifetime;
(f) to spend some time unemployed;
(g) to have a variety of job patterns.

The argument is that the period of major social, economic and technological transition associated with the post-industrial society will require young people and adults to be more adaptable, flexible and resilient, to have initiative, confidence, and the ability to cope and be creative when certainty and predictability are not part of the promise. The over-emphasis on examination success cannot be said to be best serving the needs of pupils as far as these kinds of skills are concerned. As a response to the question, "What are the skills that will allow a person to live effectively with this kind of change?", they propose the following categories of life skills:-

<u>Me Skills</u>: the skills I will need to manage myself and grow.

<u>Me and You Skills</u>: the skills I will need to be an effective member of the groups in which I will live and work.

<u>Me and Other Skills</u>: the skills I need to relate effectively to others.

<u>Me and Specific Situation Skills</u>: the skills that will be required in a variety of specific situations.

Hopson and Scally's "Lifeskills Teaching Programmes" (1981, 1982 & 1986) have produced materials to help young people to develop skills such as:-

- time management

The Pastoral Curriculum

- how to make and gain from life's transitions
- how to be positive about oneself
- how to communicate effectively
- how to be assertive
- how to make, keep and end a relationship
- how to manage negative emotions
- how to find a job
- how to study effectively
- how to prevent and manage stress
- how to learn from experience
- how to cope with unemployment

The idea is that life skills teaching needs to draw from and feedback into real life; the approach will only be relevant if it makes a difference in real situations. The aim is not merely to teach the skills a young person needs to "fit into" the world but to help him take more charge of his life or make it more like what he would want it to be. In other words, the aim is to help young people acquire the skills for autonomy.

This skills-based approach can have its drawbacks, however. Taylor (1970), for example, suggests that if we aim for "social competence" then we must describe what a socially competent person can do. This we do by describing the social roles a person may be called upon to play and then enlist the relevant behaviours, making an inventory of social skills. He suggests the following roles: father (or mother), friend, husband (or wife), neighbour, employee, trade unionist, citizen, sportsman, consumer, traveller, householder and taxpayer. It would be easy to name various others, including that of the student. Each social role, if it is played with competence, calls for certain social skills and capabilities to be exercised appropriately in certain circumstances. As Sockett (1975) asks, however, "Who counts as a good employee?" The subservient hard worker who knows his place? What makes a good trade unionist? What are the skills of being a father - and is it possible to practise them without actually being a father? Obviously role play situations can be useful here but it is unlikely that there will be common agreement to a list of skills that all fathers need. It may also be asked whether you need to be a father in order to teach about fatherhood. The point is that being a father is a much more complex activity than having a list of skills. This is not to say, however, that there is no value in <u>discussion</u> about these topics; it is simply to say that "success" in life (whatever that may mean) does not come about simply by practising a list of prespecified skills. Life is also about values and attitudes; schools need to educate as well as train.

In discussion of the content of the pastoral curriculum it is also important to consider a topic which is often ignored in discussion of pastoral care - that of "equal opportunity", particularly by gender and race. As Lang and Marland (1985) say, "the literature of pastoral care has, to date, hardly addressed itself to equal opportunity or to multi-cultural education. If equal opportunity is to be a real educational issue, it must be located in the central guidance process of the school; pastoral care". This applies whether the school is single sex or co-educational, multi-ethnic in intake or not; preparation for life outside school demands a recognition of the kind of society which pupils are to be prepared for.

2. <u>Who should teach it</u>?

The pastoral curriculum, as has been outlined, can appear almost limitless! There will certainly not be enough time for all the topics suggested to be covered in tutor periods yet, if they are considered important, these topics should be dealt with. Watkins (1985) suggests the following list of possible "locations" for the pastoral curriculum:-

- tutorial programmes
- specialist guidance lessons, such as Careers Education
- subject lessons. Can all subjects make a contribution?
- extra - timetable activities - clubs, societies, games etc.
- residential experience; work experience. These involve group or individual experiences outside the school environment.
- the "para-curriculum" of classroom and school

The Pastoral Curriculum

life (Hargreaves's "hidden curriculum").
- links with the community.

The school assembly is another "location" which can be added as it should have an integrated part to play in any pastoral curriculum (what kind of message does it convey if assemblies are regularly used for admonishment?).

The pastoral curriculum needs to work towards the appropriate use of all possible locations in a planned and co-ordinated way. Consideration needs to be given to the process of deciding "what goes where" and there will certainly be no one answer which works for all schools, staff, neighbourhoods, ages of pupils and so on. Watkins gives a useful checklist of considerations which can be employed in helping schools make their decisions and he emphasises the importance of co-ordination:-

"With numerous locations possible, numerous teacher teams engaged, and a curriculum which needs to extend across all pupils in all years, the potential for both omission and repetition is extreme".

Schools will need to decide by which mechanism this co-ordination is to be brought about.

The pastoral curriculum encompasses, therefore, more than work done in tutorial time and/or personal and social education lessons. It involves the school looking at the effects of its "hidden curriculum", as work done in tutorial time may have little effect if it is contrary to the spirit of the rest of the school organisation. It is important that skills and attitudes developed should be transferrable to all subjects and to "real" life and that "subject teaching" should indeed help young people to mature and develop as individuals who are able to play a part in and contribute to the society in which they live. Personal and social development should not be seen as a separate specialism, of no concern to those not teaching it. As Lesley Bulman (1984) put it:

"Pupils should understand the different relationships that can exist between people via studies in English, Drama, Humanities and Physical Education, at break and lunchtime, and not just during a session of Active Tutorial Work".

Bulman suggests that the pastoral curriculum is such a complicated and diverse aspect of school life that its compilation should not be left to pastoral staff alone. Pastoral staff will no doubt be instrumental in drawing up aims and objectives but at all stages consultation with Heads of Departments and other teachers on how each objective can be translated into real learning experiences is essential. As she says,

"Many of the concepts and attitudes emanating from a pastoral curriculum will be new to Heads of Departments and may be unwelcome. A joint approach from the beginning will act as in-service training for all concerned and give a much increased commitment to success".

A whole school approach such as this will make it evident that some items in the pastoral curriculum are already being taught successfully in subject lessons. Science lessons, for example, can help pupils to understand their own bodies, can help with health education, can help pupils understand the impact of science on society, and can teach pupils how to hypothesise, assess data and make decisions. The humanities can help pupils understand relationships and the different roles of women and men now, in different cultures and in the past; pupils can be helped towards becoming full citizens and to determine their own roles in a participant democracy. It will soon be evident that the kind of cross-curricular concerns enumerated earlier - values, decision-making, relationships, ability to reason and make rational judgements, concern for people, emotions, factual knowledge, alertness and determination - can be tackled in all academic subjects. A school will need to discover what is being done in academic subjects already, agree what can be done in the future, and allocate the pastoral curriculum to subjects as appears appropriate.

What then happens to tutorial time? It could logically be argued that the curriculum part of personal and social education could all be covered in academic subjects and that tutorial time could be given over to the kind of administrative tasks which have traditionally filled it in the past. If the pastoral curriculum is covered through the academic subjects, why should a structured tutorial programme be necessary? Watkins (1985) is again helpful here. He suggests three broad headings under which tasks associated with pastoral care can be classified:-

1. <u>Pastoral casework</u>, where the main focus is individual pupils, their achievement and development.

2. <u>Pastoral curriculum</u>, where the focus is on pupils and the social/personal skills and knowledge they need at school, for study, elsewhere, in later life.

The Pastoral Curriculum

3. **Pastoral management**, where the focus is on the school organisation, its staff, its curriculum and its relation to others outside the school.

It will be expected that all pastoral role holders are to be involved in all three aspects, although the balance of tasks will vary depending whether they are tutors, Heads of Year/House, pastoral deputy etc. The tutor would, therefore, take on part of the pastoral curriculum, as well as the pastoral casework and management which he has traditionally been engaged in. Where the pastoral curriculum deals with cross-curricular elements it is likely that the tutor might be best placed to teach them. An example would be study skills where the overview given in tutorial time can help consolidate the skills learnt through subject lessons. Other areas which can best be dealt with in tutorial time are:-

- where the focus is on the individual himself and the groups within which he works. This can be more easily structured in tutorial lessons than in most academic lessons.
- where the concern is the school organisation itself, how best to use it, where to go in different situations and so on. Subject teachers usually expect their pupils to know this already.
- where more time may be needed to deal with topics touched on in other subjects. An example would be "decision-making" and it would be essential to stress the importance of transfer. It will not be automatic for a pupil to transfer decision-making skills developed in, for example, History, to other areas of his life unless general principles are discussed in the tutor period.
- where matters arise which need to be dealt with. Any structured tutor programme will try to be anticipatory in its approach but topics will crop up and it is useful to be able to respond to the immediate needs of the pupils in a way which would not be possible in other parts of the curriculum. It is indeed important that the tutorial programme should not be so rigidly adhered to as to make this impossible.

Above all, the tutor will use the pastoral curriculum and the issues and discussions which it throws up to "get to know" all his group in a far more efficient way than in attempting to do this solely by one-to-one casework, important though this

37

The Pastoral Curriculum

is. The tutor will be an important link between pastoral casework and the pastoral curriculum.

3. How should it be taught?

Many schools have long taught many of the topics listed as being part of the pastoral curriculum. What is new to many, however, is the process by which it is recommended that much of this content should be taught. The emphasis is more on experiential, active learning methods and less (although not totally excluding) on the more traditional didactic method. If it is agreed that an attempt is being made to teach "life skills" then it is necessary to set up situations, which may be simulations, in which these can be practised. If the aim is to help young people to develop a set of values which are humane and thought out, situations in which some kind of open-ended discussion and research can take place need to be set up. The emphasis will, therefore, be on group activity particularly, though not exclusively, in the tutorial period. Button (1980) argues, for example, that new skills and behaviours will need to be practised in the classroom, and that what we do in the classroom must lead to new and creative action in the world outside. There is, he says, little point in approaching young people as if they were islands, to be dealt with individually. Each one is caught in a mesh of group pressures, and the proper area for "treatment" is the young person together with those who are influencing him. In school this often means his peers. Most personal difficulties run much deeper than the presenting problem and many involve basic social skills or relationships with parents, peers or those in authority. These can only be overcome in contact with other appropriate people through supportive group situations. In school the most likely group through which this could be done is the tutor group since this meets regularly, is not concerned overall with subject content and involves the same member of staff all the time. Potentially, therefore, "the key person to foster the personal development of young people is the form tutor". Within the supportive group issues can be explored, support given and skills can be practised. Active learning methods are, therefore, likely to be most efective for teaching much of the pastoral curriculum, especially as this curriculum is pupil-centred. The teachers role is that of a facilitator, and the process becomes important as well as the

The Pastoral Curriculum

content.

It is useful here to recall the philosophy of the Humanities Curriculum Project which advocated that "guidance" can be exercised in a form that is "procedurally neutral". The term "procedural" was used to indicate that "neutrality" was not to be equated with complete passivity or negative neutrality towards the decisions facing the students. The belief is that there is a way of exercising positive influence or guidance in socially controversial areas which does not involve the teacher using his authority position as an educator to take sides in favour of one side to another in a controversial situation. Experience indicates that an authorative attempt to influence thinking on such issues is likely to be counter-productive; it is also likely to hinder the development towards autonomous critical thinking. The aim of developing understanding implies the desirability of <u>discussion</u> rather than instruction as the basic educational activity. As Elliott (1975) puts it:

"To understand the issues, disputants must examine and reflect on different arguments and reasons with a view to assessing their intelligibility, and this can only be done by understanding one's own values and attitudes and exploring the relationship between these and other people's".

The importance here of the words "examine" and "reflect" cannot be over-emphasised with reference to the pastoral curriculum because such activities are essential if the learning and personal development are to be effective. It is likely that active learning methods will allow more time for examination and reflection, will encourage more <u>engagement</u> in the learning, will demonstrate that there is usually no "right answer", will encourage youngsters to value the contributions of others and will help them to learn more effectively.

The pastoral curriculum - a critique

It would be wrong to assume that there is universal acceptance of the concept of the pastoral curriculum. Hibberd (1984), for example, questions whether much which has been done informally in the past, particularly in the field of human relationships, can be done equally well formally. He argues that:

"To conduct a personal relationship on the basis of pre-specified catagories of response is not to conduct a personal relationship".

The Pastoral Curriculum

He cites the example of the carefully rehearsed responses of the door to door salesman whose conversation with a potential client hardly qualifies as a personal relationship.

"The contrived presentation of self is a presentation of a contrived self.... we may wonder to what extent simulations and role playing exercises are really invitations to insincerity, rehearsals of the contrived, turning the demanding situations of personal encounter into occasions for playing to the audience.... the individual is not and cannot ever be in the simulation as he or she is in the real situation".

Hibberd´s argument highlights some of the problems of active learning, of role play and simulation. Any role playing situation is bound to be artificial and as such it cannot be exactly like life itself. This is both its strength and its weakness: its strength because it is relatively non-threatening to the group, its weakness because it may be difficult to ensure the transfer of learning to life outside the classroom. Hibberd suggests that there are things which are not amenable to direct engagement in a curriculum, not eligible to occupy consciousness, but are nonetheless real for all that. As he says,

"...it is a common place for example that the attempt to be deliberately conscious of our own happiness is destructive of that happiness..... We can, of course, scrutinise the concept of happiness any time we wish. What we cannot do is to engage in the same direct way with happiness itself. Similarly with ´friendship´, the moment the relationship itself becomes the object of attention it begins to change".

It is possible, that to analyse why one is friendly with one person rather than another may actually change the nature of the friendship in the same way, perhaps, as the intensive study of a piece of literature may change one´s attitude towards it, perhaps for the worse. Hibberd´s objections are useful in that they highlight both the need to be clear about objectives and the need for "examination" and "reflection". In framing our pastoral curriculum we have to be careful not to trivialise it into a set of pre-specified, transferable skills which will make a "good, well-adjusted, socially-acceptable, successful, fulfilled" person as if individuals are automatons. The aim should be to help young people become autonomous persons, capable of making decisions about their participation, or otherwise, in life. This is an open ended and reflective

The Pastoral Curriculum

exercise and the pastoral curriculum should acknowledge this.

Hibberd appears to believe that the pastoral curriculum is "part of a people-making process in some way qualitatively different from a people-informing process". This is not the pastoral curriculum as we have argued it here: it is about people-making and people informing, just as all other activities in the school are designed (hopefully) to be. To suggest, as Hibberd does, that "The success of pastoral care may turn more upon the quality of the informal relationships into which the school inducts the pupil than upon the formal propriety of its pastoral curriculum" is to miss the point. The pastoral curriculum will attempt to ensure that what may have been happening informally for some will happen for all pupils, and to ensure that provision is systematically made for the personal and social education of all pupils. To rely on "informal" provision alone is actually a let down to the majority of pupils, especially if there is no discussion as to the quality of these "informal relationships".

Another problem connected with the concept of the pastoral curriculum is its relationship to "personal and social education". Are the two synonymous? The answer may well depend, as Watkins (1985) argues, on the degree to which the form tutor and pastoral staff are engaged in the activities labelled Personal and Social Education (PSE). If PSE is a cluster of subject lessons run by another teaching team, the overlap between pastoral curriculum and PSE is obviously less than if PSE is taken to include the tutorial programme or is arranged to engage the form tutor through some other means. As Watkins says, "....a pastoral curriculum which is not linked to pastoral casework is likely to be an impoverished offering..... if schools develop PSE in a relatively narrow way (and believe this is the pastoral curriculum) without engaging pastoral heads of section, a consequence is likely to be that the role of the Head of Year/House will remain subject to the forces which distort and marginalise it into a demand - led, event - led crisis management".

There is overlap between the pastoral curriculum and PSE in so far as the pastoral team has been involved in the planning, as the programme is meeting the school's pastoral objectives and as it helps in engagement in pastoral casework. If the pastoral curriculum is co-ordinated as a whole school exercise, then the overlap may well be complete.

The Pastoral Curriculum

It will be necessary for a school to set out its aims in defining its pastoral curriculum. Hamblin (1978) lists some overall objectives for "social education" as follows:-

(1) the stimulation of the development of personal values and helping pupils clarify them;

(2) the provision of the skills necessary for achievement, including study skills and the ability to plan ahead;

(3) the development of belief in the need for inner controls and the opportunity to exercise them;

(4) the promotion of a wide range of skills necessary for social competence, ranging from standpoint-taking to the management of stress;

(5) the learning of decision-making skills.

Marland (1974) also gives a useful list of aims (page 10). In short, the pastoral curriculum should help the pastoral system to support the process of learning within the school and help the development of the individual towards autonomy. McLaughlin (1983) also gives a useful perspective when he refers to those principles that "can be invoked to determine the particular problems, decisions, and adjustments facing the individual...." in the absence of which there are likely to be crises. He suggests that a curriculum programme for personal growth will need to satisfy four conditions:-

1. It will equip the young person to deal with a range of problems, decisions or adjustments that are likely to confront any person in our society.
2. The ability to deal with such "problems, decisions and adjustments" is not likely to be brought about by any other means;
3. It will ensure the school has the relevant expertise;
4. It should not get in the way of the primary task of the school, namely a liberal education.

This will involve a close examination of what problems, decisions or adjustments there are which are likely to confront young people today and in the future.

Whatever the pastoral aims may be, one of them should be to consciously set out to counter the

The Pastoral Curriculum

tendency of pastoral care systems to "pastoralise", to take on the function of deflecting, for some pupils at least, attention from the real inadequacies of the learning programmes and methods of the school. This problem, recognised by Williamson (1980) should be tackled head-on in planning the pastoral curriculum. This will inevitably raise the question of values too. As Pring (1985) recognises, pastoral care, in that it aims to promote personal development, cannot avoid ethical questions about a worthwhile form of life. What values are built into our selection of literature and other resources, into the kinds of relationships we promote in the classroom, into the proper conduct of scientific enquiry? Some of these values will be political. As Pring puts it, "....just as the extension of education was, before 1870, seen quite explicitly to be socially dangerous, so too there are those in positions of power today who express similar views (Simon, 1984). The encouragement of the spirit of criticism and of enquiry at the very time when there will be fewer occupations even for well qualified people has its social dangers. What kind of persons is it sensible to develop in the unstable economic environment we are entering into?" Education has alwyas been concerned with socialisation and social engineering. To what extent is this now a case of helping young people to face an uncertain future by "dampening down" their expectations? Is it dangerous to do otherwise? Is it socially divisive to do so? - i.e. to allow expectations to remain high for some social classes at the expense of others? How can we teach the "right" social attitudes without indoctrinating or conditioning?

There is an extent to which these questions are <u>political</u> and schools will need to come to terms with them. It is, for example, difficult to determine how it is possible for schools to decide that the teaching of "democracy" is to be part of the pastoral curriculum while at the same time adopting an authoritarian model of school organisation and teaching. It has been suggested earlier that much will depend on method, the process as well as the content, and that if we aim to help young people develop as autonomous persons, capable of independent judgement and capable of making their own decisions, then the pastoral curriculum should reflect these aims. A realistic assessment, discussion and examination of society's concerns is very much part of the pastoral curriculum; a policy of adjusting young people to an inevitable position in life is

The Pastoral Curriculum

not.

Summary

Maurice Holt (1980) has argued that comprehensive schools were set up for organisational reasons - i.e. the belief that pupils of all abilities should be educated in the same school - rather than for reasons of curriculum. Re-organisation came first and then thought was given to the curriculum. When this thought was given, the curriculum adopted was the subject-centred curriculum handed down from the Grammar and Public schools. Similarly, on the pastoral "side", the Public/Grammar school model was adopted. Both curriculum and pastoral organisations were, therefore, copied from small, selective schools and adapted to large non-selective ones, with consequent imperfections, inconsistencies, and misunderstandings. On the pastoral side it led to concern over the so-called pastoral/academic split and a concentration on an organisational/disciplinary/crisis-counselling model. This model contained within it the twin concerns of "care" and "control" which had been evident in the nineteenth century public schools and in the grammar schools, with the emphasis often appearing to be on the side of "control" if the amount of time spent by pastoral staff on this is any indication. In the 1960s as "guidance" became more of a concern and counselling courses more available a more anticipatory approach was adopted, on a one to one basis. A certain amount of literature describing good technique and good practice emerged (e.g. Marland 1974, Blackburn 1975) based largely on observation, common sense and experience but with little research evidence to back it up.

The research, when it came, was devastating in that it gave evidence which suggested what many had already suspected - pastoral systems were not actually doing what they claimed to be doing. A critique of pastoral care developed, based on the work of Best, Ribbins and Jarvis (1977, 1980, 1983), Williamson (1980), and Lang (1977, 1980, 1982), which encouraged practitioners in pastoral care to look more critically at their own work. The idea of the "pastoral curriculum" emerged and with it the potential for combining the pastoral and academic, for engaging all staff in personal and social education, and for enabling pastoral systems to achieve the purposes for which, according to the

The Pastoral Curriculum

"conventional wisdom", they were set up. The pastoral system was no longer to be a separate section of the school, required only when there were problems, but one which was to be intermingled with every other aspect of school life. The pastoral curriculum brought with it a teaching method as a more activity-based pedagogy was suggested. Button´s (1980, 1982) books and the Active Tutorial Work books gave suggestions as to how this could be done and the training programmes associated with them ensured that expertise was spread, if rather thinly at first. Some local education authorities took this up and set up support teams of trainers, an example being the Berkshire Pastoral Support Team (Goodhew and Johnson, 1985).

At the same time other initiatives such as TVEI and CPVE, which appeared at first to be instrumental rather than educational, began to develop in a way that was distinctly "pastoral", especially with their emphasis on active learning methods and career counselling. The motives behind these initiatives may well be suspect, but there is no doubt that there is a clear similarity in some of the approaches. TRIST (TVEI-Related In-service Training) has also emphasised active learning approaches, with the advantage of being school-based in many LEAs. Even GCSE, suspected as being an agent for reaction rather than change (due to its subject-based nature) has turned towards a more active pedagogy than was demanded by GCE. National and local projects on Social, Health, Moral, Political, Careers, and Pre-vocational education have elements in common which may include the concept of "negotiated curriculum" and "contract", as well as values, decision-making, relationships, cross-curricular studies, experiential learning, active learning, self-assessment, evaluation and profiling. Industrialists seem to approve too. At a seminar organised by ICI to launch Hopson and Scally´s "Lifeskills 3", the ICI management emphasised that the kind of skills they were looking for in recruits were:-

- communication
- adaptability to change
- self-motivation
- professionalism
- ability to take responsibility
- problem-solving
- initiative
- good organisation
- numeracy

The Pastoral Curriculum

- ability to work independently
- flexible
- willingness to learn
- accuracy
- ability to work in a team/several teams
- ability to work under pressure
- inter-personal skills.

It is with the development of these kinds of skills that the new initiatives and much of the work in pastoral care is involved. Much is happening to ensure that personal and social education and pastoral care should move away from its original model to a more anticipatory approach based on a combination of pastoral casework and pastoral curriculum, aided by improved pastoral management. Within this the tutor has an expanded, more important and potentially much more satisfying part to play.

Note: See Appendices 1-3 on pages 152-4.

CHAPTER 3

VOCATIONAL EDUCATION AND LIFE AFTER SCHOOL

> "....when the economy is in boom there is a tendency to allow education to fulfil the needs of individuals rather than the needs of the economy. In times of economic depression, there are pressures to force all parts of the social structure to conform to the needs of the economy. Education finds itself particularly vulnerable because it is a direct producer of a major and expensive commodity for industry - labour". (Jamieson, 1985).

The educational history of the past 150 years or so has been marked by continuing attempts to tie the education system, for some people at least, more closely to the economy and to make schools serve the needs of industry more effectively. Increasing unemployment since the mid 1970s, particularly youth unemployment, has brought about increased demands for more "relevance" in the school curriculum in order to prepare young people for industry's "needs". New initiatives to change the school curriculum - such as the Technical and Vocational Education Initiative (TVEI) and the Certificate of Pre-vocational Education (CPVE) - have been deliberately tied to the "world of work", as well as providing a general education. Integral to these initiatives is "guidance", particularly careers guidance and Social and Life Skills.

It can be argued that there are three main ways in which such pre-vocational (often called the "new vocational") courses can help young people in relation to their life after school. Firstly, they can educate them _for_ enterprise, i.e. help them develop the skills, knowledge and attitudes necessary for setting up a business. Secondly, they can educate

Vocational Education and Life After School

them <u>about</u> enterprise, i.e. help young people to understand the "world of work" and to explore wealth creation, marketing, finance, business organisation and so on. Thirdly, they can educate them <u>through</u> enterprise, promoting personal qualities such as the ability to communicate, work with others, and show initiative and drive. Insofar as such courses are able to achieve these objectives they can be said to be "enabling" in that they encourage young people to take responsibility for their own futures in a positive way. The danger is that such courses may be a subtle way of socialising young people to accept as inevitable their diminished life chances in a world in which paid employment has become more difficult to obtain.

The Move to the "new vocationalism"

Increasingly, there have been criticisms of schools and their curricula, as was evidenced by the so-called Great Debate of 1976 which, according to Benn and Fairley (1986) "marked the significant shift from support for continued comprehensive reform towards emphasis on schooling's 'relevance' to industry". Education, it was argued, was not only failing to meet the needs of industry, it was positively directing students away from it. The argument in favour of a more vocational bias is that British industry has been in a state of decline for many years so that today its performance is worse than most of its competitors. Unless as a country we can create more resources, the quality of life as evidenced in the provision of food, education, health services, transport and satisfying employment must continually decline. The root cause of this decline, it is argued, is "attitudinal"; in the words of the Director of Industry Year 1986, Sir Geoffrey Chandler, "we live in an industrial society with an anti-industrial culture". (TVEI, Insight 1986). By implication schools have had much to do with the creation of this anti-industrial culture and must, therefore, accept at least some of the "blame" for economic decline. According to Benn and Fairley the blame went to trade unions and to "the schools (but only comprehensive ones) for failing to give the right academic qualifications, or contradictorily, giving academic education rather than vocational 'relevance'".

The D.E.S. view in 1976 is evidenced in the background paper for the regional conferences during the Great Debate (quoted in Lawton, 1980): "Children

Vocational Education and Life After School

growing up in an industrial society need to understand it, and to appreciate the dependence of our living standards on the creation and production of goods and services. Those engaged in industry are often critical of the schools on the grounds that basic skills have been neglected, and that insufficient pupils pursue studies in science and mathematics; nor are the most able attracted to the manufacturing industries".
As the Green Paper (1977) put it: "There is a wide gap between the world of education and the world of work. Boys and girls are not sufficiently aware of the importance of industry to our society, and they are not taught much about it". "The School Curriculum" (DES, 1981) argued that "School education needs to equip young people fully for adult and working life in a world which is changing very rapidly indeed", while the White Paper "Better Schools" (DES, 1985), in arguing that the school curriculum should be broad, balanced, relevant and differentiated stressed that it should be designed "to develop the potential of every pupil and to equip all for the responsibilities of citizenship and for the formidable challenge of employment in the world tomorrow". The significance of "preparation for work" is further underlined: "It is vital that schools should always remember that preparation for working life is one of their principle functions. The economic stresses of our time and the pressures of international competition make it more necessary than ever before that Britain´s work force should possess the skills and attitudes and display the understanding, the enterprise and adaptability that the pervasive impact of technological advance will increasingly demand". Schools are, therefore, increasingly expected to prepare their students for "working life" at a time when work is becoming less and less available; they are also expected to ensure that their pupils develop "attitudes" and "adaptability", to cope with the situation. An implication is that schools have to socialise their pupils not only to the world of employment but also to unemployment.

Historical background

Increasingly, therefore, a more instrumental view of education has dominated offical documents since the Great Debate, at a time of economic depression. Schools have been encouraged to make what they teach

Vocational Education and Life After School

more relevant to knowledge, skills and attitudes in tune with the current requirements of industry. As Galton and Moon (1983) argues:
"In the past, the comprehensive school appeared to gear itself to meet the challenge from the pro-Grammar school lobby, in terms of the performance of a minority of its pupils in the Ordinary or Advanced Certificates of Education. Now the emphasis is beginning to shift and schools are being questioned about their failure to equip their pupils with sufficient skills to adapt to current uncertainties attached to adult life".

There is little, however, that is particularly new about this "new vocationalism"; education has always had a close relationship with the world of work. Societies tend to expect schools to develop in young people the knowledge, attitudes and skills which will enable them to contribute to the economy, while young people, and their parents, expect schools to help them enter a worthwhile job. Citing the work of Williams (1961), Watts (1986) has shown that, historically, the vocational connections of education in Britain are strong and pervasive. The first English schools, from the late sixth century, had the prime vocational intention of training intending priests and monks to conduct and understand the services of the Church, and to read the Bible and the writings of the Christian fathers. In the Middle Ages, education was organised to meet the needs of a static society based on inheritance, a society of craft apprentices, knights and clergy. The great mass of the people remained tied to the land and were not considered to be in need of education.

The eighteenth century saw the growth of a number of new vocational academies, serving commerce, engineering, the arts and the armed services. As Watts puts it: "in these academies young people were prepared for the occupation they were to assume and the place in society that it implied. The old classical education was still focussed towards the old professions for which it had vocational appropriateness - the Church, the law (and later, as it grew, towards the Civil Service)".

It was in the nineteenth century, with the advent of the industrial revolution, that, according to Williams, "the old humanists muddled the issue by claiming a fundamental distinction between their traditional learning and that of the new disciplines" - notably science and technical education. "It was from this kind of thinking", he argues, "that there developed the absurd defensive reaction that all real

Vocational Education and Life After School

learning was undertaken without thought of practical advantage". There developed what Weiner (1981) has identified as a pseudo-aristocratic, "gentrified" and anti-industrial culture which came to dominate the English bourgeoisie and which created a climate inimical to industrial and economic development.

At the same time the needs of the new factory system associated ith the industrial revolution helped bring about the extension of schooling for all. It was necessary for the new breed of employees to develop the basic skills of reading and counting, as well as the social habits desirable for repetitive work for long hours. The curriculum and organisation of the elementary schools were designed to develop these skills and attitudes; a vocational bias was, therefore, evident.

During the twentieth century, scientific and technical education gradually became established in schools and universities, the school leaving age was progressively raised, and secondary education became more widely available. The 1944 Act led to the establishment of a tripartite system - grammar, technical, and secondary modern - related broadly to the likely occupational destinations of the pupils. The system developed largely into a bipartite system, with the grammar schools preparing their pupils for "white collar" occupations, relying on the old traditional education, and the secondary moderns apparently preparing their pupils for "blue collar" occupations.

Concern in the 1950s focussed for many around the arbitrary nature of choice at eleven plus, the need for greater equality of opportunity, and with the demands for a more highly skilled workforce in an expanding economy.

The Crowther Report (1959) highlighted the fact that at the ages of 16 and 17 over half the boys and nearly four-fifths of the girls got neither full-time education nor day release and the Minister of Education was called upon to "re-affirm his intention to implement at the earliest possible date the provision of compulsory part-time education for all young persons of 16 and 17 who are not in full-time education". The curriculum offered should include four particular strands:

1. An appreciation of the adult world in which young workers suddenly find themselves.

2. Guidance for them in working out their problems of human relations and moral standards.

51

Vocational Education and Life After School

3. Development of physical and aesthetic skills.

4. A continuance of basic education, with a vocational bias "where appropriate".

The clientele were to be prepared for a future in which "there may be less need of ´skill´ in the old fashioned sense of the word; what will be needed in ever-growing volume will be the quality that can perhaps be described as ´general mechanical intelligence´". As will be seen later there are similarities in the curriculum suggested and the target group for modern developments in pre-vocational education. The Crowther Report reflected what was essentially a divisive system; there was an educational elite who received "academic" (but no vocational) education, a "training" elite who received vocational training, often in apprenticeships, and an unskilled mass who received no education or training. This latter group were to be helped to cope with their lot: the Report gave no indication that the proposed changes should bridge the divide. There is now concern that this divide is not only still with us but that much of what is currently being proposed will serve to perpetuate it.

Towards a common curriculum

In the years following the Crowther Report, with comprehensive re-organisation, attempts were made to bridge the divide, particularly with "open access" sixth forms following the raising of the school-leaving age to 16 (a Crowther recommendation). Many comprehensive schools, based originally on the concept of "equality of opportunity", came to accept Daunt´s (1975) "second view" of comprehensive education:
"It is a principle of equal value.... the guiding defining principle of comprehensive education is that the education of all children is held to be of equal value".

Changes within comprehensive schools - common curricula for all abilities, mixed ability teaching, faculty organisation and integration of subjects, mixed classes for "craft" subjects, the development of the pastoral curriculum - often reflected a movement towards that principle. The Certificate of Secondary Education, with its link with ´O´ level, was seen as giving access for many to the academic hierarchy in a way that was not possible before. The

Vocational Education and Life After School

development of what has been called the "cafeteria curriculum" - usually comprising a core of English, Mathematics, P.E., plus a free choice of five or six other subjects from a list of perhaps 20 - raised doubts about curriculum balance for the 14/15 year olds concerned, however. H.M.I., in the first of the "Red Books" (1978), postulated eight areas of experience - aesthetic and creative, ethical, linguistic, mathematical, physical, scientific, social and political, and spiritual - as "one way of encouraging coherence and balance in the overall curriculum of individual pupils". The conclusion was that 70%-80% of the time available between 11 and 16 years of age should be devoted to the "curriculum entitlement" (the eight areas of experience), the remaining time being allocated for optional components. "The School Curriculum" (1981) also accepted that:

"The curriculum offered by a school, and the curriculum received by individual pupils, should not be simply a collection of separate subjects; nor is it sufficient to transfer, with modifications, the ideas about the curriculum in the separate selective and non-selective schools of an earlier generation into the comprehensive schools attended by most pupils today..... there is an overwhelming case for providing all pupils between 11-16 with curricula of a broadly common character with substantial common elements".

Denis Lawton (1983) suggests that education is concerned with making available to the next generation what we regard as the most important aspects of "the culture" and that "because schools have limited time and resources, the curriculum should be planned carefully to ensure that an appropriate selection from culture is made". He argues that culture can be sub-divided into eight systems - social, economic, communication, rationality, technology, morality, belief, and aesthetic - and that an adequate selection must include all eight.

The Hargreaves Report, "Improving Secondary Schools" (1984), proposed that there should be core subjects (62.5%), constrained options, and free options in an attempt to provide a balanced and motivating curriculum.

The theme of these reports and studies is that there should be a common entitlement for all secondary school pupils and that comprehensive schools should ensure that this is on offer. The difficulty is, however, to decide how this relates to "subjects" on the timetable and in ensuring that what is taught is "relevant". It seemed to many that, despite the plethora of curriculum documents, little change actually took place in schools. The subject-centred curriculum, geared towards academic qualifications, still prevailed. The H.M.I. report (DES, 1979) on secondary schools in England and Wales found that the style and quality of work in the 4th and 5th years of secondary schools were dominated by examination requirements. Teachers, knowing that their effectiveness was likely to be judged in terms of examination results, tended to adopt teaching styles they considered necessary to promote examination success. This tended to encourage teaching which, in the view of H.M.I., was "unsound, unstimulating and ineffectual".

It was not surprising, however, that comprehensive schools should adopt the academic curriculum of the grammar schools. Many of the secondary modern schools had already moved in this direction as they had found a number of their pupils to be capable of passing Ordinary level examinations. For many, the development of the comprehensive school now meant that the "race" was open to all as pupils were not prematurely excluded at the age of eleven. This "race" was for access to "white collar" occupations for which traditional academic qualifications were still required. Watts (1985) argues that while the content of the curriculum became less relevant to the occupations which many pupils would take up, its connections with the world of work grew no less. Its basic rationale was that it enabled <u>selection</u> to take place. "If secondary schools in particular no longer <u>prepared</u> pupils for particular forms of employment in such an overt and direct way as hitherto, what they did continued to be influenced and justified by the extent to which it determined <u>access</u> to employment". It was this desire to prepare pupils for access to "white collar" jobs, together with the changing nature of the skills demanded by industry, which helped to make the school curriculum less "vocational" in a direct sense. The result was, therefore, to extend to almost all pupils an academic curriculum very like that previously offered to only the minority in grammar schools (and to a few in secondary moderns), a curriculum which many young people came to regard as irrelevant to their immediate and future interests and which labelled them as failures. Since the system was designed to provide access for as many as possible to "white collar" jobs, and since for many these were

Vocational Education and Life After School

perceived as being occupations in the professions rather than in industry, it was inevitable that schools should be accused of having an anti-industry bias. Ironically, however, industry still demanded of its recruits the traditional examination passes and this ensured that the system would continue. Industry's recruitment policies therefore helped to perpetuate a system of which it claimed to disapprove.

Education and employment: functions

Watts (1985) distinguishes four functions which educational institutions, can perform in relation to employment:-

1. <u>Selection</u> - education has increasingly taken on, as has been seen, the functions of allocating and selecting as well as training individuals for their adult roles.

2. <u>Socialisation</u> - education can influence students' attitudes to the world of work and to their function within it.

3. <u>Orientation</u> - concerning deliberate curricular interventions designed to help students to understand the world of employment, and to prepare for the choices and transitions they will have to make on entering. The two facets of this function are "Careers Education" and "learning about work".

4. <u>Preparation</u> - promoting the acquisition of specific skills and knowledge which students will be able to apply in a direct way after entering employment. On the whole the tendency until recently has been to limit the extent to which schools have been involved in vocational preparation.

These four factors have all played their part in the educational process over the past 150 years but, as has been indicated, the emphasis has changed according to perceived economic needs. The effect of unemployment and an economy in decline has been to sharpen the debate about their relative importance as an attempt is made to harness education in attempts to halt economic decline. It has also helped to draw greater attention to the orientation and guidance function of education in relation to employment and this has become central to YTS, TVEI and CPVE. The

Vocational Education and Life After School

debate here concerns the extent to which this function may be an attempt to reinforce the process of socialisation - what Roberts (1977) refers to as "anticipatory socialisation" to a reality in which people's lives are determined largely by the opportunity structure - or, alternatively, the extent to which it is designed to make the whole process more visible and therefore open to questions and deliberation - to make it a learning process rather than a conditioning process. While "guidance" has assumed a more central role in the curriculum, particularly in the pre-vocational initiatives, it would be wrong to assume that there is universal agreement as to its prime function.

The target group for the "new vocationalism"

The target group for many of the schemes associated with the "new vocationalism" of the curriculum, excepting TVEI, are the bottom 50% or so, the group identified by Crowther as receiving no education at all after leaving school. By 1980 the situation was no different to that at the time of Crowther. In January 1981 58% of 16-19 year olds were in jobs (or were unemployed) with little or no systematically planned training or further education; this compared unfavourably with France (19%) and Germany (6%). In his Graham Clark lecture for 1982 (reported in the Times Educational Supplement, April 1982) Sir James Hamilton, permanent secretary at the DES, in outlining the part education should play in "peace and prosperity", argued that "the most troubling problems relate to that 40% at the lower end of the academic scale. Many of them finish their 11 years of schooling so antipathetic to education that they have no wish whatever to return to it; they constitute the major part of the 16 to 19 year olds who are either in work, but without education, or are out of work; they represent the most vulnerable fraction of our community in terms of work for the future..........it is they who are going to find it increasingly difficult to equip themselves for employment in the manufacturing industry of the future, and they who may find that opportunities for employment in the service industries have already been pre-empted by their better qualified fellows. For them the need for a more imaginative school and post-school education becomes the sharper". Among the "remedies" suggested are a move towards a pre-vocational approach particularly for the "crucial" years of 14-16, a

Vocational Education and Life After School

"more sensitive" record of their achievements than is provided by formal examinations, and "a clearer path up the ladder from unskilled to skilled to technician to professional" after 16. This "special needs", "remedial" treatment seems a far cry from a "common curriculum entitlement" and suggests a pre-vocational education for "bottom 40%" while the rest are prepared for technician to professional level, with some hoped-for ladder in between. Gleeson (1983) and Green (1986) have argued that this approach has already led to a three-tier structure in Further Education, Tier 1 comprising students on full-time higher, technical and business courses (BTEC) and those doing GCE ´O´ and ´A´ levels, Tier 2 including those on craft courses and junior clerical courses and Tier 3 including those on a disparate array of courses such as CPVE and YTS. Green foresees the potential collapse of Tier 2 "pressaging an imminent polarization in the structure that corresponds with an increasing division in society between intellectual and manual labour". In addition, he says, the essence of both the practical skills training and the social and life skills training in YTS is not the mastery of technical skills but the inculcation of appropriate work attitudes and social and communication skills - "all of which rank high in MSC priorities for unskilled work.... What counts now in youth training is the cultivation of adaptability and the willingness to accept the fact that many working lives are likely to consist of a succession of unskilled jobs". In this analysis YTS is "more a question of ´keeping them off the streets´ than a matter of extending rights to comprehensive education and training".

The "new vocational" initiatives have been designed to affect the curriculum in the 14-18 age range and guidance has been given a particularly important place in them. This is natural as it is an age range in which important career decisions have to be made by all pupils. For "new vocational" pupils, guidance, particularly Careers Education, appears to gain in importance because of the different arrangements which typically apply to the courses. Consortium arrangements may bring pupils into contact with staff from more than one school or college and this has implications for both staff and pupils, not least in record keeping. Co-ordination becomes very important as staff and pupils react to a variety of learning situations. Work experience, mini-enterprises and the involvement of adults other than teachers also have implications for guidance as pupils have to make sense of a variety of messages coming to them from a number of different adults, apart from the influence of their peers.

Wallace (1985) reminds us that the process of guidance consists of four main elements:

1. <u>Appraisal</u> - enabling the individual to discover information about himself - his abilities, interests, needs and values - and thus build up a realistic picture of himself. This self-assessment needs to be a continuous process, not a once-and-for-all part of a 3rd Year careers programme.

2. <u>Information</u> - providing the individual with facts, and also the ability to research the facts, about future alternatives.

3. <u>Orientation</u> - assisting the young person with adjustment to new situations and helping him to anticipate any difficulties which might occur at transition stages.

4. <u>Counselling</u> - the establishment of a professional relationship with an individual in an interview in which a young person is encouraged to clarify needs, hopes and problems and to plan appropriate steps to meet them.

Guidance of this kind is particularly important at fourteen plus, sixteen plus, on course, and at the end. It will involve helping young people to make choices - often of totally new subjects and courses - taking into account their own abilities and interests, and the likely vocational implications. Sex-stereotyping will need to be tackled to combat attitudes of pupils and parents towards certain occupational areas which inhibit the former from making certain choices. On course, guidance will continue to be needed to help pupils to appreciate and understand the idea of transferrable skills, to help them review their own progress, to support them in their encounters with a variety of adults, to prepare them for work experience and to help them to adapt to a variety of institutions. At the end they will need to be helped to progress to new situations outside school. All of this has implications for school management as decisions have to be made concerning factors such as time, staffing and in-service training, bearing in mind that none of this is applicable only to students on the "new vocational" courses. All students need similar

Vocational Education and Life After School

guidance, and its establishment has become increasingly evident in schools. What is different, however, is that guidance is written into the syllabus, something which is not a feature of GCSE and ´A´ level. It is, therefore, even more important for teachers and lecturers to be clear as to the purpose of the guidance that they are giving, as the development of the "new vocationalism" raises important questions for the education service. If education is to "relevant", what is meant by relevance? To whom must it be relevant - to the needs of employers, governments, society, or the young people themselves? Can it be made relevant to all of these? If not, whose needs should take priority? Is it possible to identify these needs (employers, for example, are not a homogeneous group)? Who should do the identifying? Whose interests is education serving? Are we in the business of raising aspirations or "dampening them down" to "realistic" levels in an age when there are fewer opportunities? What part should educational guidance and counselling play in this situation?

Jamieson (1985) points out that the simple assertion that a "vocationally orientated curriculum" would serve best does not gain much support from overseas evidence. In America, he says, Norton Grubb and Lazerson (1981) have shown that their own education-industry movement has paralleled our own and that vocationalism has largely failed to meet the economic requirements of employers, while in Japan there is a high performing economy with a school curriculum which is "narrowly academic and is not much influenced by considerations of vocational application". (Watts, 1984).

Fundamental, therefore, to the "new vocationalism" are questions concerning the aims of education for young people in a changing society. Hopson and Scally (1986) argue that our task should be to help young people to become "self-empowered": "We believe that current social, economic and political patterns are not there simply to be accepted and conformed to. Lifeskills is not about teaching young people to be acceptable to employers, thus promoting conformity and accepting the status quo. Social skills teaching can suggest an approach to education which Paulo Friere called a process of domestication. Teaching lifeskills, developing self-empowered individuals who "own" their own skills and believe in their power to influence and change what is not acceptable, is a fundamentally different approach".

Vocational Education and Life After School

"New Vocational" Initiatives

The Crowther Report reflected a divisive view of education. The establishment of comprehensive education and the corresponding move towards a common curriculum entitlement for all children of compulsory school age, represented a potential to end these divisions, although this did not always happen. More recently, a desire to make the secondary curriculum more "relevant" to the perceived needs of many of the pupils and to the needs of the economy, has led to the development of "pre-vocational" courses for those in the 14-18 age range. A number of commentators (e.g. Benn and Fairley et al, 1986; Walker and Barton et al, 1986) regard the "new vocationalism" as restoring division into the education system, with different types of curriculum organisation for different "types" of pupil, with the curriculum for the academic elite remaining much as before. The rest of this chapter will involve a discussion of the way in which TVEI, CPVE and YTS fit into this argument.

"A Basis for Choice"

The seminal document which influenced the direction which the pre-employment courses have taken was "A Basis For Choice", produced by a study group of the Further Education Curriculum Review and Development Unit (F.E.U.) in 1979. The report was concerned with full-time courses for young people who entered further education after leaving school and who needed something other than GCE studies or programmes preparing them for specific occupations. The group's deliberations, although intended for Colleges of F.E., were also relevant to the secondary sector and had implications for all institutions involved in 16 plus education.

The study grouo was aware of the danger of proposing yet another course as this would only add to the existing confusion: "Our aim, therefore, has been to put forward proposals for a <u>course structure</u> which would help to reduce the confusion which exists in this area, and not simply add to the plethora of available courses". The report argues that "a major contribution towards the fulfilment of our criteria would be made by the existence of a common core in the various kinds of provision on offer", and that courses must have transferability (i.e. students should learn generally applicable skills and capacities and have the ability to transfer them);

Vocational Education and Life After School

vocational orientation and flexibility to cope with variations in vocational commitment between students, individual changes, local variation in the needs of industry and the prospects of employment; and a "fairly wide" spectrum of student ability and attainment.

The suggestion was that the general objectives of the basic course should be categorised under three main headings:-

1. <u>Core Studies</u> (60% of the course) - defined as "those studies to which all students of this age should have right of access, and that learning which is common to all vocational preparation, including induction".

2. <u>Job specific studies</u> (20%) - "that learning which is particular to a given job within a vocational sector".

3. <u>Vocational Studies</u> (20%) - "that learning which is particular to a given vocational sector".

Thus a student might study division of labour as a general concept (core), learn how jobs are structured within the building industry (vocational) and investigate the kinds of work and skills required of a plumber (job specific).

The core as a whole was expected to provide opportunities for young people to develop practical numeracy, their ability to communicate, their ability to learn from study, experience and colleagues, social skills and understanding in a variety of contexts, self-confidence, self-awareness and adaptability, a variety of physical and manipulative skills, their awareness of various technological, environmental, political, economic and aesthetic factors which affect their lives and to provide a basis from which to make informed and realistic career choices: "and it should do this in the context of their intention to enter into the world of work in the near future". It was felt that "participatory learning activities will be more effective than passive reception of subject matter" and that there was a need for "counselling of various kinds - in connection with career choice, learning styles and the ability to transfer skills and learn from experience, for instance". As far as assessment was concerned it should be "formative wherever possible, thus allowing both the student and teacher to benefit from feedback from each other". This would involve

Vocational Education and Life After School

profiling.

"A Basis For Choice" included, therefore, most of the elements which are typically expected in pre-vocational courses - a core, a cross-curricular emphasis, participative learning, a vocational focus, transferable skills, awareness of the social, economic, political and technological environment, a link with local job opportunities, a "framework" (not a course) to allow local flexibility, guidance and counselling, personal and social education/ lifeskills, and profiling. Most of these were not typically included in ´O´ and ´A´ level and the Times Educational Supplement (October 1980) pointed to the danger of creating two different and divided streams: "It is important to insist that the more systematically young people are steered away from the ´academic´ stream and towards vocational education and training, the more essential it is to open up opportunities for recurrent education later on. At the centre of these proposals should be a belief that many young people who leave school labelled ´CSE grades 2-4 have undeveloped potential which will come out later in working life´". The FEU agreed with this sentiment in their response (1980) to the consultative document: "Examination 16-18", stressing the importance of "the recognition of vocational preparation as a legitimate educational process in its own right which should somehow be rewarded". It also suggested, referring to ´A´ level students, that "our most academically advanced young people are also entitled to experience the process of vocational preparation, albeit at a level appropriate to their needs". Pre-vocational education should not be confined to the "less able". Wallace (1985) notes that Sir Keith Joseph, then Secretary of State for Education, referring to the proposed GCE A/S level, TVEI, CPVE, and YTS, said that "the Government aims to define standards of performance and to develop a system of certification which can be applied to both YTS and to pre-vocational and further education. As Wallace says: "the schools will note that all four phenomena started or were planned in the same academic year of 1983/84 and may wonder whether it is sensible to design different routes and then try to make them coherent as a secondary activity. We may also note the absence of GCSE and GCE A/S level from Sir Keith´s aim to achieve coherence, and may be anxious about the possible re-emergence of a duality of routes which we have been trying to discard".

Vocational Education and Life After School

THE TECHNICAL AND VOCATIONAL EDUCATION INITIATIVE (TVEI)

TVEI is unique among the "new vocational" initiatives in that its target group, although as yet not the majority of its clientele, is young people of all abilities. It arose out of a desire on the part of the government to tie education more closely to employment. The White Paper "Better Schools" (DES, 1985) declared that "the linkage of education and training ......should have preparation for employment as one of its principal functions. Such preparation should help young people to make themselves more suited to likely patterns of employment. It will therefore be necessary to resolve the issue of how best to fit work-related skills within initial full-time education". It goes on to argue that:

"The resolution of this issue and of the link between education and training centre on the 14-18 age range, and have to embrace the work of the schools and of the colleges of further education, and the needs of industry and commerce". TVEI was established to meet these issues: "The TVEI embodies the Government's policy that education should better equip young people for working life. The courses are designed to cater equally for boys and girls across the whole ability range and with technical and vocational aspirations, and to offer in the compulsory years a broad general education with a strong technical element followed, post 16, by increasing vocational specialisation. The course content and teaching methods adopted are intended to develop personal qualities and positive attitudes towards work as well as a wide range of competence, and more generally to develop a practical approach throughout the curriculum". It is argued that "the projects are innovative and break new ground in many ways, being designed to explore curriculum organisation and development, teaching approaches and learning styles, co-operation between participating institutions, and enhanced careers guidance supported by work experience, in order to test the feasibility of sustaining a broad vocational commitment in full-time education for 14-18 year olds".

The launch

In November 1982 the Prime Minister announced the Government's intention to launch an initiative to stimulate the provision of technical and vocational

Vocational Education and Life After School

education for young people. By September 1983 - only ten months later - students in 14 Local Education Authorities had embarked on the first year of the TVEI programme. The purpose of this pilot scheme was to explore and test methods of organising, managing and resourcing replicable programmes of general, technical and vocational education; and to explore and test the kinds of programmes, curricula and learning methods required for success. The M.S.C. set out five principles:-

- the Commission would work through L.E.A.s.

- individual projects would adopt different forms according to local circumstances.

- the Commission would consider projects based on existing facilities as well as new ones.

- young people's participation in the scheme would be voluntary.

- the precise curriculum should be a matter for local determination with certain general criteria/ guidelines applying nationally.

The criteria

According to David Young, then Chairman of the MSC, the objectives were: "First, our general objective is to widen and enrich the curriculum in a way that will help young people to prepare for the world of work, and to develop skills and interests, including creative abilities, that will help them lead a fuller life and to be able to contribute more to the life of the community. Secondly, we are in the business of helping students to 'learn to learn'. In a time of rapid technological change, the extent to which particular occupational skills will be required will change. What is important about the initiative is that youngsters should receive an education which will enable them to adapt to the changing occupational environment".

A National Steering Group drew up the criteria for the initiative:-

- equal opportunities for both sexes.

- four year (14-18) curricula with progression from year to year.

Vocational Education and Life After School

- encouragement of initiative, problem-solving abilities and personal development.

- balance of general, technical and vocational elements throughout the programme.

- vocational elements broadly related to employment opportunities.

- planned work experience from the age of 15 onwards.

- periodic assessment of progress and record of achievement on completion.

- regular educational and careers guidance.

- students to prepare for one or more recognised qualifications.

- entry open across the ability range.

- students to take part with others in the life of the institution.

- flexibility between courses within the programme.

- provision for movement in and out of the programme.

Importantly, the initiative was well-funded right from the start, at a time when local authorities were being forced to cut expenditure on education. As chitty (1986) puts it, "the large amount of MSC funding......made TVEI an irresistible gift.....there was money for new equipment, new staff, new curriculum development, new in-service training and new building to house TVEI units in schools". Nationally, by 1985 about 3% of all 14 year old pupils spread over 8% of secondary schools were involved.

TVEI and central control

TVEI marks an important step in the intervention by central government, through the MSC, into the one time "secret garden" of the curriculum. Impatient at the limited response to the Great Debate and numerous curriculum documents and guidelines, central government has devised new ways to manage curriculum change by appealing directly to local authorities and schools. The new pattern is for government to set aside funds for particular policy developments, supplying guidelines and inviting bids from L.E.A.s, who then may invite bids from their own schools. This model is being used for in-service training developments with T.R.I.S.T. (TVEI-Related In-Service Training), followed by G.R.I.S.T. (Grant-Related In-Service Training). As Fiddy and Stronach (1986) point out "This kind of categorical funding (as opposed to block funding) can be represented as a move towards centralisation in terms of innovation, because the government acts rather more directly to influence policy at local levels. It can also be represented as a kind of devolution with L.E.A.s and schools carrying much more responsibility for innovation, and for detailed curriculum and assessment development".

TVEI and curriculum change

The advocates of TVEI point to the great need for change in the secondary curriculum. As Mike Davies, Deputy Director of Stantonbury Campus remarks, "Children born today will still be in the school system in the year 2000; what is our version of the society into which they will emerge and contribute? If we accept that we are in transition from an industrial age to a media age, then what is the school's response? Do we organise the school day, the timetable, the classroom, movement in the corridors, as a mirror image of forty years ago? Are we really playing an integral part in the development of the young person or are we in danger of cocooning ourselves in an island of obsolescence, unaffected by the advance of time or change in the wider world beyond?" (TVEI Insight, March 1985). When David Young introduced the initiative he declared that he was only trying to give the education service a badly needed short sharp shock, accompanying it with the threat that "the MSC has the power and the authority to open its own establishments, so let me say at the outset that we have no intention of doing that as I believe and hope we can work as partners with the local education authorities. If that did not prove possible, then we might have to think again". (T.E.S., November 1982).

Wallace (1985) points out that technical studies had no place in the selective grammar school, a lowly

Vocational Education and Life After School

place in the secondary modern school, and have been struggling for space in the comprehensive schools. In their early development, comprehensive schools were aware that they were judged, not by pioneering curricula, but by their ability to do for the ablest child what the grammar school could do. He notes that "it has been the politics of the comprehensive reform which has debased the role of technological, business and vocational studies, and has ensured that a curriculum, established largely for nineteenth century aristocrats, has passed almost unscathed through the grammar to the comprehensive school". The argument is that this mould needs to be broken by the establishment of technological as well as other vocational studies as essential elements in the curriculum of all children, covering the full range of ability. "Without the impetus of government supported change", he argues, "we shall continue to direct the ablest away from technological studies and in the direction of what we mistakenly think of as untainted, pure education". TVEI is thus seen as the pilot project to initiate this change.

There is much to be said in favour of this argument. The low status of engineering and technology in this country in comparison to Germany, for example, has long been evident. It seems unlikely, however, that TVEI in itself will effect great changes unless it can actually attract students of all abilities. TVEI experience so far has shown that there is a difference between being open to all abilities and actually attracting all abilities. Able students are aware that Higher Eduction institutions put great emphasis on the importance of traditional academic qualifications, as indeed do many employers. As Benn and Fairley (1986) point out "with the exception of the proliferation of business and technological courses for further and higher education and attempts to limit the study of the humanities - the educational institutions, examination paths, curriculum and professional training of Britain's ruling elites, academic or social, are not being much disturbed by government policy". Chitty (1986) quotes the Chief Master of King Edwards School, Birmingham, as saying in a T.V. discussion in 1985 that his school did not do TVEI because his was a school for "academic boys hoping to go to university". TVEI of itself cannot bring about a change in attitudes.

Vocational Education and Life After School

TVEI and general education

An additional fear is that TVEI represents in practice a new kind of "relevant" course for lower achievers; that it will help to bring about differentiation within the institution by setting up a different class of student. TVEI appears to have been the brainchild of David Young, one-time Chairman of British O.R.T. (Organisation for Rehabilitation and Training), an organisation which tends to concern itself with motivating "non-academic" pupils by its concentration on vocational instruction. Benn and Fairley argue that "the humanities and social studies are being progressively squeezed into an ever smaller space. Components of vocational or training schemes ensuring the development of the skills of critical enquiry - particularly those associated with high-level general education - are being reduced or atomised under the banner of the 'new vocationalism'". As White (1982) puts it "The great mass of the population are thought to need education that fits them for certain kinds of jobs and gives them no deeper understanding of society as a whole than their particular role requires, while those who belong to the ruling elite are held in need a more rounded education". It should be said, however, that courses fitted in with TVEI criteria would not of necessity result in the kind of curriculum which White describes. It is, however, a possibility and one of which those involved in Guidance will need to be aware.

TVEI can be seen as a response to the accelerating changes in society and in the field of employment. The education service has been responding to these changes - as the developments associated with the pastoral curriculum indicate - but change is not always easily brought about and progress has inevitably been patchy. TVEI provided funds and a stimulus for change, but gave little time for planning or in-service training. Many authorities and schools felt that they were rushed into making their submissions and they have had to work out the implications of TVEI as they went along, year by year. In-service training directed at TVEI staff has taken them out of school, provoking potential tensions, as has the divisive nature of the scheme, with cash, equipment and staff being directed into favoured areas at the expense of others. TVEI can sit uneasily in option blocks, in competition with more traditional subjects, and it can also lead to distorted timetables for individual pupils. A 4th

Vocational Education and Life After School

Form timetable comprising English, Mathematics, Physics, Chemistry, Computing, Electronics, Applied Science and Technology, Lifeskills and Physical Education - followed by a student in one TVEI school - (Berkshire TVEI Project Progress Report, March 1985) - can hardly be said to be giving the young person a good general education. It should be said, however, that his was an early and untypical example and it does emphasise the importance of guidance. TVEI is expected to provide breadth and balance while broadening the curriculum to include the technology of society today, the antithesis of premature specialisation. This will not happen, however, without careful planning and guidance.

TVEI and equal opportunities

Despite the importance attached to equal opportunities, it does not appear that TVEI has broken down sex stereotyping in a significant way. Surveys in a number of areas have indicated that boys are still more likely to take TVEI subjects than girls and that they choose "boys" subjects within it. (Herbert, 1986). As Herbert points out "the label 'technical and vocational' is in itself an inherited gender-loaded title" in that they are words which often evoke masculine reference points. In the Berkshire TVEI project Progress Report for October 1985 it is stated that "staff are saddened by the repeated confirmation they receive during the options process that we are up against deep-seated pressures in the form of both parental and peer group expectations. One school reports open parental pressure on children to make stereotyped option choices at the individual family interviews held in school". As a result a number of steps were being taken to try to achieve a better balance, including an intensification of counselling of pupils and parents at the option stage. As with YTS and CPVE, the problem is much wider than TVEI and is one that needs to be tackled throughout the life of the school as a whole. As Herbert says: "In terms of sex discrimination it is a question of teachers perceiving the problem as significant before they might be expected to investigate alternatives. This is a necessary baseline position before the process is worth attempting". In bringing about change Fiddy and Stronach (1986) stress two ground rules:-

1. "Create" an awareness of the problem before you

Vocational Education and Life After School

address its solution.

2. If policy precedes awareness, then entrenching of attitudes will ensue.

All of this has obvious implications for guidance in relation to the curriculum.
It is to be hoped that the experience of TVEI will provide models for tackling the "Equal Opportunities" issue and help to "create awareness", even though the TVEI criteria do not actually mention the issues of "race" and "class". The TVEI experience could, perhaps, also lead to a broadening of education away from a subject-centred orientation. As Mike Davies put it (1985) "the next century will demand new skills and abilities, not just those to do with operating a computer, but also being aware of the growing powers of the media, bias and prejudice. Alongside a new technical and economic literacy, we shall need a new political literacy as well as a greater community and social commitment. Tomorrow's world is not simply a hundred best ways of using the chip, its about creating a new humanity and harmony". Moves towards providing this kind of curriculum in TVEI in Birmingham are described by Brandes and Ginnis (1968).

Certainly the MSC see TVEI as an important factor in changing the school curriculum. In his speech to the summer meeting of the Association of Colleges of Further and Higher Education (reported in the T.E.S., June 1986) Geoffrey Holland, the director, said that it was crucial to maintain the momentum of TVEI, which he called "the most important curriculum development in a long time". The MSC has been arguing forcefully that the scheme has already proved itself and that the "urgent need" to reorient the education system towards industry requires a start on a full-scale national programme without delay. The Government accepted this argument and announced that TVEI would be extended over the next ten years to make technical and vocational courses available, though not compulsory, to all 14 to 18 year olds. The Times Educational Supplement reported (1st August 1986) that "it is now clear that there is no question of the TVEI being handed over at the end of the pilot programme to the education service to run, as Lord Young, hand-on-heart, has repeatedly promised in the past...... The education interests involved are no longer challenging this...... they are content that the actual decisions as to the criteria and the vetting of proposals are in the hands of the TVEI

Vocational Education and Life After School

national steering group which they dominate; and that the MSC co-ordinators on the ground are helping rather than hassling the schools and colleges running the courses". The model of centrally devised criteria and priorities, backed by central control of funds, but locally devised schemes of work and syllabuses, seems to be here to stay.

The Certificate of Pre-vocational Education

The development of CPVE was also much influenced by "A Basis For Choice" and followed the guidelines laid down in the D.E.S. booklet "17+: A New Qualification" (1982). This document argued that single subject examinations were not appropriate for the target group, defined in negative terms as "young people of widely varying ability but usually with modest examination achievements at 16 plus, who have set their sights on employment rather than higher education, but have not yet formed a clear idea of the kind of job they might tackle successfully, or are not yet ready to embark on a specific course of vocational education or training". It seems clear, therefore, that CPVE was planned for non ´O´ level students right from the start and was intended as an alternative. As a Joint Board (City and Guilds and BTEC) document indicates, however, they do not take this limited view: "It is intended to be available for all young people, certainly up to those studying for ´A´ level". The experience of schools working with the City and Guilds ´365´ course, designed on ABC lines, suggests the necessity of "selling" it by linking it with other examinations, such as ´O´ level and it is likely that there will be a similar experience with CPVE even though "Better Schools" (1985) still insists that it is for "those young people who stay on full-time in either schools or colleges for one year after the compulsory period and who are not pursuing CSE or ´O´ level (or in due course GCSE) qualifications with a reasonable hope of success, and do not have a clear vocational aim in view". The White Paper makes it clear that CPVE is to have a "strong element" of general education, as well as a progressively sharpening vocational focus and that "for the most part CPVE courses will involve not the teaching of separate subjects but the development of skills, knowledge and attributes across the areas covered by each course". In line with ´ABC´, CPVE provides a curriculum framework, not a course. This framework has three components, the Core, Vocational

Studies and Additional Studies. The Core and Vocational Studies are to occupy a minimum of 75% of the course time, and these two components are to be co-ordinated and integrated so that students see them as a coherent whole rather than as separate subjects. Students may use the remaining time either for Additional Studies or for further development of the Core and Vocational Studies. It is compulsory for institutions to provide Additional Studies but they are not obligatory on the student. The core competences are grouped in ten areas: Personal and Career Development; Industrial, Social and Environmental Studies; Communication; Social Skills; Numeracy; Science and Technology; Information Technology; Creative Development; Practical Skills; and Problem Solving. These ten areas should not be taught as separate subjects; they are expected to be integrated with each other and with other parts of the programme. The Vocational Studies which are to provide the focus for the development of the common core competences, are organised into five main "categories"; Business and Administrative Services; Technical Services; Production; Distribution; Services to People. They are to be taught through a modular structure. Learning strategies are to include activity-based learning, work experience (a minimum of 15 days) and Guidance and Student Support. The Joint Board CPVE criteria (1985) state that:

"A system of student counselling and guidance is an integral part of all courses and must be closely related to formative assessment and the profiling system. It will include regular meetings between the student and a personal tutor at which problems and progress can be reviewed and future patterns of learning agreed. This involvement of the students in the planning of their own programmes and learning contributes to course integration by helping them to perceive the course as a coherent whole".

CPVE tutors are, therefore, expected to be able to adopt a student-centred approach, to negotiate the curriculum, negotiate formative and summative profiles, review progress periodically, use activity-based methods and encourage students to take responsibility for their own learning. In addition they must also ensure that a programme of Careers Guidance is included as well as all that is involved in a properly planned work experience programme. CPVE has been planned initially as a one year course for 16-17 year olds but in its Consultative Document (1984) the Joint Board invited comments on the potential for a part-time CPVE (to become part of the

Vocational Education and Life After School

two year YTS?) and on the place of CPVE within the concept of pre-vocational education pre-16 (to link with TVEI?). This presages the introduction of a comprehensive system of pre-vocational courses in schools which will effectively provide a parallel structure to the 16 plus. A Government working party report maintained that pre-vocational courses are applicable to all pupils, including those studying primarily for GCSE but, according to the Times Educational Supplement (18th July 1986): "most of the members accept privately that the main function of the courses for the time being will be to provide an alternative general education for pupils who do not respond to traditional teaching". The working party says that pre-vocational courses for the 14-16 year olds should be judged by standards "as rigorous as those being set for the GCSE". It does not prescribe one form of curricular structure but does say that pre-vocational education cannot be provided as a single subject course. Since the advocated course structures for the pre-vocational courses are substantially different from those for GCSE, A/S level and 'A' level, the real dangers of a divided curriculum and premature specialisation are evident. Also problematic are the links between the various courses and progression to the world of work.

The various Joint Board booklets - e.g. the Consultative Document (1984), the Criteria booklet (1985), and the Core Competences booklet (1985) - make little mention of equal opportunity although Jack Mansell, Chief Officer of the F.E.U., does say in his introduction to "CPVE in Action" (the evaluation of the 1984/85 pilot schemes), that "the report hopefully shows that CPVE has the potential to provide a balanced curriculum of general and vocational development for a wide range of students, irrespective of ability, gender and background". The evaluation found that as far as ability was concerned entry qualifications (as a measure of ability) varied from none to a clutch of 'O' levels; however, the majority of students had a few CSEs at grades 2/3/4. It also showed that sex stereotyping clearly existed in the choice of vocational subjects, when choice was given. Few teachers or students had anything to say about racial stereotyping. Some black students, however, saw some vocational options - e.g. a particular vocational study of services to public - as unsuitable for them on the grounds that progression into some courses or types of employment was closed to them on account of their colour. Some considerations of sex and racial stereotyping and discrimination were also significant in work experience. The pilots did not feel that they were influenced by gender or racial bias, but that the stereotyped views of a wider society were imported into CPVE courses by students and staff. As the evaluation notes: "In these cases....... students' views reflected their perception of the reality of the world of vocational training and employment rather than implied criticism of the CPVE course itself. It is, however, possible that pilots might have done more to counteract such views".

As far as Guidance, Counselling and Assessment were concerned the evaluation found that teachers (and no doubt students) were uncertain about the mechanics of profiling, that time was needed for personal review sessions and that students have a need for guidance pre-course, during the course, and post-course. Curiously, nothing was said about the need to develop counselling skills and the skills of negotiation.

Although there was a 40% drop out during the year, largely because students obtained jobs, student reaction to the courses was generally favourable with 70% of students saying that they would recommend CPVE to their best friends and 80% considering that the programme had assisted them with their career plans. They valued vocational studies and when asked what changes they would make in re-designing their programme many suggested more vocational studies and less core. Other aspects valued were practical work, visits and work experience, and the change of atmosphere from that associated with traditional classroom teaching. Less valued was a too theoretical approach to teaching - too much talk by the teacher and too little practical work. Clearly the participative approach coupled with a vocational focus appealed to the students and motivated them to work. However an evaluation by Gary Storer (T.E.S., June 1986) found that "most students felt that CPVE failed to prepare them for F.E., and colleges' recognition of CPVE is very patchy". This situation will not be helped by BTEC's introduction of a new first certificate course aimed at students of "good average ability", not yet qualified to embark on vocational courses for the council's national awards. It will, it seems, be the normal route for entry to the national awards and the "more appropriate" route for those who have taken pre-vocational courses already. As Storer says, although CPVE was intended as a preparation for all the routes a person might pursue, "it seems to be really a preparation for YTS

Vocational Education and Life After School

or work". One reason suggested for some dissatisfaction with CPVE among students, reflected in the 40% leaving in the pilot year, was that the 6th Form was too late a stage for pre-vocational courses, with students expecting more vocationally relevant education. It is possible, therefore, that as TVEI expands and pre-vocational education moves further down the age range, the long term future of CPVE is in doubt. As Michael Duffy (T.E.S., June 1986) put it, referring to the new BTEC first certificate course: "Can it be that the co-partners, who so stridently demanded to be midwives to the CPVE, are going in for infanticide?" These will become important issues as far as Guidance and CPVE are concerned.

The Youth Training Scheme (YTS)

The Youth Training Scheme was set up under the auspices of the Manpower Services Commission. The MSC argued in its document "A New Training Initiative" (May 1981) that to take advantage of our opportunities we need to adopt the new technologies, that young people faced special difficulties because of the rise in youth unemployment, that apprenticeship was proving increasingly inadequate to present and future needs, that at school young people were being less well prepared than they should be for working life, that only 50% or so continued in full-time education or further vocational training, which compared unfavourably with our major foreign competitors, and that we needed a more highly trained workforce. The document suggested, for example, that in many parts of the country local communities were in decline "because they lack the skills" required to attract inward investment or enable new local enterprise to flourish. It stated that "the new markets and technologies require a more highly skilled, better educated and more mobile workforce in which a much larger number of professional and technical staff are supported by a range of more or less highly trained workers who perform a range of tasks and who are involved in a process rather the repetitive assembly or manufacture of a part of a specific product". The Youth Training Scheme was to provide the training for the "more or less highly trained" workers, to ensure that the 50% of 16/17 year olds not involved in further education and training should be so, and, presumably, to ensure that the "communities in decline" acquired the requisite skills.

The Youth Task Group report (1982) said the aim was "to provide....... a better equipped, better qualified, better educated and better motivated workforce". It was also designed to eliminate youth unemployment as the Youth Task Group stated that it wished to ensure that "all young people under the age of 18 have the opportunity either of continuing in full-time education or of entering training or a period of planned work experience combining work related training and education". Drawing heavily on "A Basis for Choice" the group said that the content of the course should be:- induction and assessment of the trainee's skills; basic core skills; experience of the world of work; training in "families of occupations"; process skills; advice and support throughout the programme. There would be a record of achievement for all trainees at the end. The scheme was to provide a minimum of three months off-the-job training, either in Further Education colleges or employers' premises. It was anticipated that there would be a link with the new 17 plus examination and the Group wanted schools "to ensure that the school curriculum develops the personal skills and qualities as well as the knowledge needed for working life", adding that "appropriate levels of competence in numeracy, literacy, oral expression, social relationships and understanding of the world they face outside education will mean that young people are more likely to gain from the scheme we are proposing". In short, the argument was:-

1. There had been a rise in youth unemployment.

2. We need a more highly trained workforce.

3. Youth unemployment and the decline of communities was due to lack of skills.

4. These skills should not be narrowly vocational.

5. Schools ought to be doing more, and will be expected to ensure that their pupils have adequate preparation for YTS.

The report was stronger in argument than it was in evidence. Dan Finn (1986) suggests that the MSC's "interventions have become monetarism's panacea, obscuring the manifest economic failure of government policy and suggesting instead that the causes and cures for unemployment are to be found, not in the economic and social system, but in the capacities and skills of individual workers".

Nevertheless, the Youth Training Scheme was launched nationally in 1983, initially as a one year scheme but extended in 1986 to two years. The MSC booklet aimed at young people outlined its aims: "YTS offers broad training to help you get off to a good start in working life; it will help you be more attractive to employers and give you a certificate to show what you can do, which will be useful when you apply for a job afterwards". There would be, as the Task Group had recommended, a minimum of thirteen weeks off-the-job further education, direct practical experience, training in a group of skills related to an area of work, social and life skills, and advice and help about how to make the best use of the scheme, each trainee being attached to a member of the training staff to review progress on a regular basis. Each trainee was given an allowance of £25 per week: as David Young put it (Guardian, March 1985) "Young people are not worth much when they leave school, although their worth increases with the right training. But they have no God-given right to a good wage". It is not surprising, in the light of this, that the most consistent criticism trainees make of YTS concerns the low level of the allowance, which has not been linked to inflation.

Equal opportunities were to be maintained. The MSC announced, "YTS will, of course, be open to all young people within the range of eligibility regardless of race, sex or disability....... and the Board will look to all parties involved in the preparation and delivery of individual programmes, and in the recruitment of young people to avoid discrimination and to accept the principle of equal opportunity for all". (MSC press statement, July 1983). It was, perhaps, inevitable that YTS would not achieve the goals it set itself. In attempting to provide over 400,000 places rapidly it was inevitable that quality would vary, and organisational divisions within YTS tended to make this worse. The simple division was Mode A for large employers and Mode B schemes to be run largely by voluntary bodies and local authorities. Apart from the fact that a large number of local authorities operate under Mode A schemes there are other divisions within Mode A, for example between mere "work preparation" schemes and schemes which provide genuine skill training. There is also the division between employer-based schemes, where young people are trained on the premises, and those schemes where the managing agent is a college or a Private Training Agency (PTA). According to Pollert (1986) the PTA schemes now account for between a quarter and a half of all Mode A schemes, depending on the region. In addition there is the Large Companies Unit which often provides the most prestigious training of all and is not required to submit to monitoring by local boards. As Finn (1986) argues, "What has emerged is a two-tier system within the YTS scheme. The majority of trainees are offered ´work preparation´ while the minority are involved in the process of real vocational training on the lines of a first-year apprenticeship".

It was natural, in these circumstances, that employers should use YTS as a screening process. Indeed, the excess of "trained" persons over available jobs will be a continuing feature of the scheme as employers are encouraged to take on more trainees than they have openings for and are paid to do so. With up to half of those on YTS schemes not expected to get permanent jobs at the end it is difficult to refute the suggestion that for many employers it provides a pool of cheap trainees from which they can pick and choose for permanent work. In this situation the guidance and counselling provided is likely to be of the kind that stresses conformity to employer standards, "creating a new generation of workers who will be pliant, adaptable, non-unionised, and grateful for any job whatever the conditions" (Finn, 1986), a workforce - in the words of the Chancellor of the Exchequer - "with the right skills; one that is adaptable, reliable, motivated and is prepared to work at wages that employers can afford to pay". (Nigel Lawson, Budget speech, March 1985). The off-the-job training is not intended to be used to promote discussion on political issues, moral problems or controversial current affairs. Initial Department of Trade guidelines specifically excluded YTS trainees from considering "matters related to the organisation and functioning of society in general". As Finn argues, it appeared that these young people could learn how to complete application forms but they would not be allowed to discuss why they were unemployed! These guidelines were toned down but the incident does suggest that work socialisation was considered to be more important than participatory citizenship.

As far as equal opportunities is concerned Pollert (1986) and Solomos (1986) have shown that racial disadvantage and discrimination has not been overcome by YTS, something which an MSC document acknowledged (1985): "discrimination exists in society and in employment and YTS experience is reflecting that..... it would be wrong to look to training schemes of any kind to solve more widespread problems of discrimination in employment". This lack of positive action is also reflected in the approach to the issue of gender stereotyping and Marsh (1986) and Buswell (1986) have shown that YTS has made no difference to the disadvantaged position of women and their narrow options at work.

A problem for the MSC is that with so many employers and so many schemes it is difficult to monitor adequately what is happening, particularly as it relies on the co-operation of employers to provide training places. Finn quotes a survey from Income Data Services Ltd in 1984 which concluded that the "MSC is in no real position to police the scheme thoroughly" and that its "staff have neither the experience or time to monitor schemes adequately". The establishment of the Training Standards Advisory Service, to provide an independent source of advice and guidance on the quality of training under YTS, in September 1986, can be expected to improve matters but it is anticipated that there will only be 40 advisers to cover a shceme which provided 360,000 places in 1985/86. (T.E.S., August 1986). It is, perhaps, a sign that YTS is not fully achieving its aims that the MSC announced in August 1986 that "all over the country vacancies for skilled jobs are not being filled" (BBC news). Paul Ryan (1984) has shown that YTS offers little prospect of solving the chronic problem of training for key skills. Skill training is dependent on employers´ policies and the subsidy available under YTS does not come near to meeting the real cost of apprenticeship training. Finn quotes the Engineering Industrial Training Board which pointed out that the recruitment in 1985/85 of 3,000 first year technician apprentices compared badly with the nearly 6,000 required merely to replace natural losses. Finn suggests that the acute shortages in specific skills which are currently restricting the pace of technological change can be largely blamed on industry itself as it cut back on both capital investment and training during the recession. "Even now", he says, "according to the Industrial Society, two thirds of British employers spend less than 0.5 percent of their annual turnover on staff training". It seems clear, therefore, that new measures are needed if this skill shortage is to be overcome; one way would be to ensure an upgrading of skill training in YTS.

Guidelines on the design of YTS training (MSC

1982) made specific recommendations about guidance and social and life skills. For instance, guidance should aim to promote self reliance and needs to be a continuous process. Indeed, FEU (1985) describe guidance and counselling as part of learning and the skills used within guidance work as relevant and useful to the whole student-centred approach to education. Consequently, such skills are essential parts of the tutor's repertoire. Special emphasis is given, in the guidelines, to co-operation between all those involved in the guidance process, i.e. Careers Service, colleges, youth workers, managing agents, etc. In practice, it is the Careers Service that plays a significant part in this process, with other provision varying enormously (NYB 1983). Lack of training in guidance is also a major handicap, as regards managing agents. Little distinction was often made between guidance, assessment, and record/review of progress. Similarly, NYB (1983) reported that "social and life skills is destined first to change name, then to be reduced and eventually to disappear" from YTS.

There is also the important issue of guidance prior to entering YTS. Evidence suggests that boys are more likely to receive counselling as distinct from information, as opposed to girls (Fawcett Society 1985). This report indicates unsatisfactory guidance provision at school, subject choices made by girls that limit their opportunities, sex stereotyping whilst on YTS, and much criticism of the scheme by trainers. Clearly, there is a good deal of improvement required in the area of guidance and personal development provided by YTS. The Careers Service is of key importance at all stages, and generally provides good support to YTS trainees, but its resources are limited and there is a clear need to strengthen the guidance provided by the other agencies involved.

Conclusion

The years since the Great Debate have seen a number of significant changes in education and training, the most significant of which has been the increasing central control over schools and of the curriculum. The Great Debate itself and the various curriculum documents produced were attempts to influence the curriculum. The abolition of the Schools Council and its replacement by two nominated bodies increased the government's influence over education as did the

Vocational Education and Life After School

restriction of funds for education given to the L.E.A.s. Short of money, the local authorities bid for what they could get from TVEI with varying degrees of enthusiasm, and this gave the government an improved means of bringing about educational change; the existing means had had little effect. A technique of requiring authorities to "bid" for funds from central government through the MSC evolved, thus giving the government greater control over how the money was spent. The MSC was thus used as the agent for increasing government involvement in education and for changing the process of changing schooling itself. The possible closure of the Further Education Unit (T.E.S., August 1986), the autonomous DES-funded agency set up to review the further education curriculum and other aspects of provision, could be seen as the stifling of another independent voice which has been critical at times of government policies.

One effect of this increased central control has been to "vocationalise" the curriculum in schools and colleges, often hastening developments which were already happening. It had long been argued, often by teachers, that the secondary school curriculum overemphasised the "academic" at the expense of the "technical and vocational" and that schools have to be geared more closely to the needs of industry. The knowledge, skills and attitudes that young people were taught in schools were often inappropriate both for the great majority of them and for what Britain and the economy required. Young people were typically leaving secondary education ignorant, if not contemptuous, of the economic basis of the nation's wealth, the way the country makes its living. As well as being ill-disposed towards industry, what they had been taught in school fitted them ill for the knowledge and skill requirements of the modern economy (Dale, 1986). In this analysis, it was essential to put some kind of vocational education into the schools.

At the same time progressive educationists were noting the restricting influence of examinations and the single subject curriculum, advocating more active, experiential learning, drawing up profiles and counselling and pastoral curricula. They, too, were antipathetic towards "over academic" learning and the traditional "transmission" model of teaching, whose meaning is best conveyed in the idea of "instruction", with all its authoritarian and undemocratic connotations of experts and passive receivers. There were already strong advocates in the

81

teaching profession for the teaching of personal and social education, for schools/industry links, and for more "relevance" for education to help young people understand the society of which they are part. Hargreaves (1982) called for the abolition of examinations and for the development of modular courses more geared to the needs of the pupils and the community and the "Manifesto for Change" (T.E.S., January 1981), with 32 distinguished signatories, urged that a "vigorous transformation of secondary education is of immediate and profound importance for the future of young people and our society".

The progressive model had, therefore, much in common with the "new vocationalism" during these years, creating a receptive clientele when the various schemes were introduced into schools and colleges. Educationalists need to consider, however, whether as Green (1986) puts it "good ideas are being used for bad ends". The most obvious "bad end" is the possibility of a divisive organisation of the curriculum. Chitty (1986) argues that "We can assume that in the future the vast majority of 16-18 year olds, and perhaps up to a third of 14 year olds will be ´trained´, while the top 20% will continue to be ´educated´ via GCE grades in the GCSE, ´A´ level, higher education and the professions. Those in between will get a variety of pre-vocational ´options´ in schools, followed by the ´option´ of a variety of narrow vocational courses after 16". Teachers will need to consider whether aspects of the "new vocationalism" are aimed at socialising young people to accept their fate, a life of unskilled work with periods of unemployment for the majority, marginalising still further the disadvantaged.

H.M.I. (1977) defined a common curriculum as a "body of skills, concepts, attitudes and knowledge, to be pursued, to a depth appropriate to their ability, by all pupils in the compulsory years of secondary education for a substantial part of their time, perhaps as much as two thirds or three-quarters of the total time available". The idea of a broad, balanced and non-segregated curriculum which avoids the perils of premature specialisation, and where the common elements amount for a significantly large proportion of the pupil´s working week should not be abandoned lightly; neither should Daunt´s principle of equal value as a comprehensive ideal. On the other hand schools do need to meet the challenges of a world outside them which is changing rapidly. CPVE, TVEI, and YTS are not in themselves necessarily a threat to a coherent comprehensive education for all;

Vocational Education and Life After School

it is the way in which they may be used. There is little doubt that much of what these initiatives have brought into the curricula of schools and colleges has been for their enrichment. What is needed is a coherent system which allows for the fusion of "academic" and "vocational" education for all and which aims, in the term used by Hopson and Scally (1986), to "self-empower" all young people. They argue that greater self empowerment leads to a more altruistic society:

"There has been some particularly interesting research which demonstrates clearly that the more self-empowered people are the more likely they are to help others, and tend to be more competent as helpers. In other words, the more people take charge of their own lives, the less selfish they are likely to be. This is hardly surprising. People who are low in confidence, anxious, and feel powerless are likely to be too involved in their own problems to have time to help other people with theirs. Their attitude is more likely to be one of "you´ll have to put up with it, there´s nothing you can do". This is confirmed by the further research findings (Phares, 1976) that more self-empowered people are more committed to social and political action than less self empowered people. The message from the research studies is clear - the more young people feel that they do have some power to influence what happens to them, the more they will use that power for the benefit of others and the community".

The lesson for teachers is also clear; young people need to be helped to become more self-empowered. This could well be where the influence of Guidance and Counselling in the new initiatives, central as these are to their planning, will be so important.

Pring (T.E.S., June 1986) has argued that there is an unnecessary polarisation over preparation for the world of work. On the one hand, he says, preparation for the world of work has become one of the least controversial cliches that now characterise the deliberations over aims and content of the changing secondary school curriculum. Connections are made between school curriculum and what students are expected to be doing subsequently, as though the education value of learning is extrinsic, lying in the acquisition of skills or knowledge or attitudes which will prove beneficial to the future employer. On the other hand there are some, he says, who "would rather see schools like monateries, undisturbed in the pursuit of learning or in the enjoyment of poetry by the distractions of economic life or of adult preoccupations. Childhood and youth come but once, and the prospect of entering the world of work should not overshadow them". The intrinsic value of education is emphasised.

This polarisation is, he argues, "very odd". "The preparation for the world of work, if that is interpreted in the sense of specific vocational skills or of deferential social attitudes, would not be an educational task. It would be a form of training that ignored the broadening experience that leads to critical appreciation and to a deepening of understanding. Schools are not training workshops". However, he argues, we cannot find acceptable a philosophy of education which, in the pursuit of learning and of moral and aesthetic appreciation, ignores the very context which needs to be understood and responded to. The broadly conceived liberal education that seeks the expansion of understanding in its various forms should seek, too, that understanding of the economic and industrial base upon which the possibilities of pursuing educational studies depends. "Above all", he says, "it should seek to help each individual find his or her own personal stance in relation to that economic and industrial base - personal, moral, and political attitudes which are well informed and which arise out of self-knowledge as well as knowledge of the world of work". Perhaps the solution lies he argues, in focussing on personal development: "Is it too much an act of faith to argue that the best preparation for the world of work lies in the increased powers of mind to reflect, to think, to enquire, to solve problems, to speculate - the very qualities that a liberal education at its best should be pursuing". This does not allow for any complacency for those in education; they have the task of interpreting and deciding on what that liberal education "at its best" should be in the face of contradictory messages from outside education and uncertainties within. In this fluid situation the role of "guidance" could be crucial.

CHAPTER 4

CAREERS EDUCATION UNDER PRESSURE

> "All education theories are in the end political theories. But careers education is directly concerned with the relationship between education and the allocation of life chances, and is therefore political in a particular direct sense, especially in a society which is characterised by considerable variations of remuneration status between different occupation".
> (Watts and Herr, 1976).

Although this was not always the case, today careers education is one part of the pastoral curriculum that has been widely accepted as essential. It is seen as relevant, useful, and non-controversial, providing a clear cut link between education and the "world of work". Significantly, within the last three years, its importance within the curriculum has been acknowledged by the MSC through the outline of required "good practice" from schools participating in TVEI. However, what actually constitutes "good" careers education is much less easy to identify and there is no real agreement on the content, the approaches to be adopted, or even the objectives of such a programme. Indeed, "Better Schools" (DES, 1985) comments that there is "little evidence of agreed curriculum policies..... in particular on such pervasive matters as careers education".

During the last decade, there has been a considerable amount of discussion about careers education and the DES has contributed to this debate. In a discussion document (DES 1983), the aims of careers education have been clearly set out.

"Careers education and guidance is not a subject, but a process on which a school needs to have a policy. Designated careers teachers, subject specialists and teachers in their pastoral role should contribute. Careers education and guidance should help individuals:

- to become interested in and aware of opportunities in education and training, in work and in adult life generally.

- to understand themselves in relation to these opportunities, their strengths and weaknesses, interests, values, qualifications and circumstances.

- to make informed, reasoned decisions.

- to make transitions, in particular from school to the next stage.

It is necessary to prepare young people to cope with unemployment by developing their personal resources and by informing them about helping agencies and teaching them how to use these. They need knowledge of the labour market, including opportunities outside the formal economy and they need to be aware of the impact of technology and the changing nature of work".

As Rogers (1984) points out, these aims embody life skills which include decision making, learning, coping, leisure skills; awareness of self including values, interests, strengths and weaknesses; cultural transmission, in other words "the base needed to make sense of the world which each generation inherits and to enable them to change it". Whilst the aims set out above are very comprehensive, it is worth considering these in relation to the principles for a school guidance programme set out much earlier by Barry and Wolf (1962).

(1) The programme should serve the pupil, not the teacher at the school.

(2) It should start with a realistic approach to the individual. This is a call for integrating careers education into the mainstream of personal development work carried out by the school.

(3) The programme must broaden the interests, experiences, learnings and aspirations of the pupils. This is very challenging as it means pupils need not just learn passively but must be active and have the opportunity to experience and to broaden their self

knowledge and their knowledge of the working world.

(4) The programme should be judged by how well it meets the pupil's needs. Thus evaluation, based on consumer opinion, is necessary.

(5) What is done for one need not be done for all. This is not a plea for the academically able to be excused careers education! It is a reminder that pupils' needs vary and, as far as possible, careers education should cater for this.

(6) The programme must be professional. It means that careers teachers require training and sufficient resources to do their work properly.

Although written in the context of the United States, these six principles highlight some of the underlying issues any careers education programmes; such as whose interests does the programme really serve and how can it best be presented and delivered. Law (1981) suggested a typology for understanding the different provision of careers education. Where Careers Education is not permitted to interfere with the existing curriculum, but is given official prominence he categories as "cosmetic". In practice, there is no real commitment to it. Another type of careers education emphasises links with employers in order to maximise the chance of the school being able to claim success for their pupils in gaining employment. Little attention may be given to whether this employment is actually best suited to the pupil's needs and aspirations.

These two approaches do not involve any real changes in curriculum priorities, neither does the third, where careers education is a supplement. In this instance, the school provides a resources centre, e.g. careers room or part of school library for pupils to consult at break periods and after school. Interviews and perhaps some group work will be carried out. Careers education becomes a "real" subject when regularly timetabled. Once this has happened an evolution often takes place. The programme provides a general focus on self assessment and occupational knowledge, including presentations by employers. In time, this may develop into a more varied and challenging programme involving more "participative" activities, typified by the Schools Council careers education and guidance project materials. This different style of learning and the challenging nature of the material can put careers

education at the "margins" within the school.
More recently, Hamblin (1986) draws attention to the fact that "careers education, when interpreted strictly, is an ambiguous and misleading term". He points out that rational planning of a career is, in practice, only relevant to the middle class or able pupil. The reality for many pupils, based upon their parents´ experience of work is one of putting up with frustrating jobs by evasive and outwitting tactics. He adds, "their tolerance in the face of careers education which contravenes their knowledge of reality is amazing".

The structure and content of programmes

In practice, careers education can mean many different things. There is no agreed or co-ordinated programme that applies across even a small number of schools. (Watts and Law, 1977). This situation is made even more diffuse by the lack of an examination structure to formalise the topic around an externally influenced curriculum. Whilst it is possible to examine programmes developed at national level such as the SCCEGP, it is not possible to say how far such material is being used in schools. Very often a patchwork quilt approach is adopted by a school piecing together material from various sources to produce a careers education programme that lacks coherence. Recently, a number of programmes of life and social skills (Hopson and Scally, McGuire and Priestley) have become available and are being used in some schools. These serve to blur the lines of demarcation between careers education and social education, and illustrate a more general trend to link careers education into the wider pastoral curriculum.
Careers education has found it difficult to establish an identity for itself for various reasons. It is not an "academic subject" and is not part of the examination "race" which has now been made such an important part in determining the standing and success of a school. There is no initial training of teachers in this area of the curriculum, which leaves it without a firm foundation.
Careers teachers have lacked training, status and financial reward. Crucially they have also been denied time and resources, as well as a departmental base. Sometimes, there has been confusion over their role in relation to careers officers, and on occasions, as a result, rivalry and misunderstanding has arisen. Faced with this unenviable and basically

untenable position, the quality of careers education has come in for a good deal of critical comment by employers and to some extent, pupils and parents.
Careers education has become more developmentally orientated and there is evidence to suggest that this developmental orientation is indirectly the result of Donald Super's work (Roberts, 1977, Daws, 1977). His theory of career development became influential in vocational guidance circles in the sixties and formed a rough and ready theoretical basis for careers education in Britain. This is despite the fact that his life stages suggest that the tentative stage extends to the age of 17 and transition lasts from 18-21. For those pupils who leave at 16, the notion of making a firm occupational choice seems unrealistic in Super's terms. This has been criticised as a theoretical approach more applicable to the States than to Britain (Roberts, 1977). Arising from Super's original propositions, careers education in Britain has tended to focus upon an extended programme over 1-3 years prior to the school leaving age. The programme lays emphasis on self exploration and awareness whilst providing for some reality testing, though the provision of a variety of activities including role play, work experience and counselling.
Thus, the early preoccupation of vocational guidance with matching the individual to a job has given way to careers education concerned with concepts such as self awareness and opportunity awareness, decision-making and preparation for transition (Watts and Herr, 1976). By laying considerable emphasis on self awareness, careers education has brought itself into contact with other programmes that exist in many schools such as Active Tutorial Work, although this does not mean that co-ordination necessarily takes place.
Self awareness emerges in a number of forms in careers education programmes. In most cases, self assessment is encouraged by various means e.g. JIIGCAL and more broadly, the issue of relating to others might be raised. In recent years, social skills has become a rather hackneyed term, but despite this, much useful attention has been given to the area of interpersonal skills. Finally, the broader issues of different lifestyles has become more commonly explored in schools. This might well be related to other crucial issues as unemployment and gender.
Opportunity awareness has been a concern of vocational guidance since the very early days. An

emphasis was given to providing appropriate information on jobs and the employment market. In careers education, this has been extended to include an examination of the nature of work, job satisfaction and why people work. Work experience has become more common and is seen by many schools as an important direct learning experience. The notion of widening pupils´ awareness of work opportunities has been criticised as unrealistic (Roberts, 1977) and dysfunctional. The practice can certainly be questioned in a time of high unemployment. Indeed, the issue of unemployment is one that schools in general find difficult to deal with (Watts, 1984).

Decision-making has obvious relevance in careers education, although its importance would seem to diminish in those parts of Britain where the Youth Training Scheme is the only choice available. The importance of decision-making has been extended to consider both options at 13 and other choices made in life after school. Finally, preparation for transition is a topic that has concerned schools for some years. Helping pupils to complete application forms and to present themselves more effectively at interviews are examples of this practice. Other sorts of preparation include information about tax, insurance, unemployment benefits, trade union membership.

Bates et al (1984) has charted the development of Careers Education in Britain. She describes the last decade as one in which "it became more difficult for careers education to face both ways, with related repercussions for the progress of the ´development model´". These repercussions are reflected in four different themes: Firstly, the social change theme is one that has been raised by various authors. (Hopson and Hough, 1985; Watts and Herr, 1976). It identifies inequalities in work as being an integral part of the social structure and perceives careers education as having a role in assisting change which will eventually result in youngsters benefiting from a more equal working structure.

The second theme is concerned with individual adjustment. Watts and Herr, (1976) use the term social control to describe the process that takes place "In careers education terms, it requires restricting in a subtle way the nature of occupations presented to each student and placing some emphasis on the dignity of all work". Roberts (1977) has been particularly critical of the developmental approach in careers education and seen it as making adjustment to the harsh reality of the employment market much harder. "No harmony is guaranteed between individual's aptitudes and occupational requirements, and guidance may have the effect not of closing but of widening the gap. Refusal to recognise the limited role that careers guidance can play will not change other social institutions for the better. The net result may be that young people will become less able to adjust to the world as it is".

The question of alternative roles constitutes the third theme and arises from the fact of growing, large-scale unemployment. This has undermined the notion of paid employment as being central to people's lives, especially those of men. Daws (1977) stated that "Careers Education programmes are primarily concerned to help young people determine the kind of life that they want and in that context to consider which among the jobs realistically available to them offers the most likely and approximate fit to what they seek as a style of life and as a satisfactory way of 'making a living'". Daws was emphasising paid employment as one aspect of "lifestyles", as did Super (1981) in his "life career rainbow" which identifies 9 potential roles which can be occupied at some stage of life. Super states that these roles are conducted within 4 principal theatres: home, community, education and work, thus putting work on a par rather than of prime importance. These authors are effectively down-grading the place of paid employment from its central all-embodying position defined by the Protestant Work Ethic. This process began before mass unemployment made this inevitable and reflected a recognition that for many workers, paid employment could never give them much satisfaction beyond a wage.

Encouraging individuals to adjust to unemployment undoubtedly raises some questions about the desirability and morality of this approach. Unemployment certainly means accepting a low standard of living, and in addition can lead to ill health and isolation. Of course, unemployment does not effect the population as a whole evenly; there are important regional, social class, ethnic and gender differences. It is important to ask if these are factors that should be accepted and adjusted to or should they be challenged. Equally, it is clear that the unemployed can be helped to cope with this situation in various ways which may involve individual, group or community action (Dauncey, 1981; Watts, 1984).

Careers Education Under Pressure

Unemployment

High levels of youth unemployment have inevitably caused much debate about the role of schools in relation to this problem. Watts (1984) suggests that there have been three broad effects on education. Firstly, unemployment challenges the legitimacy of schooling which was based upon "the incentive to persuade adolescent pupils to attend, to behave well and to work hard in school" in order to gain qualifications which would lead to a good job. Secondly, the growth of youth unemployment has been attributed, in some quarters, to the deficiencies of schools, who were not preparing their pupils adequately for the rapidly changing demands of the economy. For instance, the MSC (1975) stated bluntly "the social environment in a number of schools with more emphasis on personal development and less on formal instruction has been diverging from that still encountered in most work situations, where the need to achieve results in conformity with defined standards and to do so within fixed time limits calls for different patterns of behaviour". Thirdly, education has been seen as a means of responding to youth unemployment, by providing activities for youngsters who would otherwise have been unemployed.

If schools are seeking to deal with the issues raised by unemployment, careers education provides an obvious focus. However, when Watts (1984) sought information from schools who were responding creatively to the problems posed by unemployment, there was no response. After further investigation he was able to describe the activities of three schools, chosen for their apparent diversity. The schools had taken steps to pay attention to "official" alternatives to unemployment, to developing leisure activities, to developing survival skills for use if unemployed, to raising awareness of the economic and political causes of unemployment and to considering the future of work. All three schools were in areas of high unemployment, and some moves were being made to make provision for local unemployed youngsters.

Unemployment is a key social issue that can and ought to be represented in the school curriculum. A number of curricula objectives have been outlined by Watts (1984). These can be described in terms of skills or awareness raising. For example, the question of teaching employability skills has been under discussion for some years. This encompasses job search and acquisition skills, as well as less clear-cut skills concerned with job retention, and social skills designed to increase employability. Survival skills for the unemployed are less commonly taught. These include knowledge of benefits and redundancy rights as well as skills in claiming rights and in handling a limited budget. Watts includes references to the psychological effects of unemployment and to the social pressures it brings. This can be seen as much less easy to deal with in a classroom, but could lend itself more readily to some creative work in drama for example.

Leisure skills might be seen as an obvious area to be covered, but schools have tended to deal with this in an ad hoc fashion, often leaving this area of the youngster's life to chance. Informing them of facilities is important, but the active cultivation of a wide range of interests could be seen as a vital function of education. Finally, opportunity-creation skills are geared towards self employment, which may take several forms, either individually or collectively.

Awareness can be raised in several senses. For instance, adaptability can be encouraged by making youngsters aware of jobs that may not immediately appeal to them, or which may mean travelling further afield or even leaving home. Contextual awareness has to do with considering the issue of responsibility for unemployment. This can be seen at one extreme as resulting from individual inadequacy and at the other as purely a failure of society to provide enough jobs. Issues such as technological change, various political and economic solutions, and the possible alienating effects of work are certainly relevant to youngsters.

Clearly there is a basic dilemma when dealing with the issue of unemployment in schools. By encouraging youngsters to come to terms with unemployment, does this then lead to an acceptance of their position which makes it harder to seek and find employment at some point in the future? The particular stance taken by schools will depend on the predominant attitudes and values towards unemployment and to the future of employment. Unemployment can still be seen as less desirable than having any sort of employment. Similarly, there are widely differing views about the likely chances of increased future employment which will inevitably colour the way in which schools will deal with the question of unemployment.

Careers Education Under Pressure

Equal Opportunities

Inevitably careers education is concerned with the issue of equality. Within schools, this tends to be implicit and perhaps even hidden but it remains central to the actual distribution of young people into post school opportunities. Social class, ethnic origin and gender are the major social divisions leading to inequality in British society. In recent years there has been a growing awareness of the need for schools to consider sexism and racism and this has had an impact upon careers education. The sexual division of labour remains largely unchanged, reinforced by a sexual division within the curriculum. Increasing attention has been directed to these issues, especially by feminists, and by such statutory bodies as the Equal Opportunities Commission (EOC) and some interesting initiatives have arisen.

It is in considering a key issue such as sexism, that it becomes clear that careers education needs to be closely integrated into the pastoral curriculum, as so many topics relate to the whole "life style" rather than just paid employment. An obvious example of this would be subject choice in the 3rd year. Decisions made at this point have a direct and important impact on later occupational choices. For instance, girls are less likely to choose the physical sciences and technology and this has a severely restricting effect on the range of occupations they can hope to enter. Indeed, occupational choices are being formed early in the young person's education and to be effective, careers education must take account of this and provide positive learning experiences for both girls and boys.

As Whyte (1981) also points out "boys suffer from sex stereotyping in the curriculum and in careers guidance. Boys receive from school very little support for the social roles most of them later encounter as boyfriends, sharers of flats, husbands, babysitters, householders..... This is sad because it implies a possible frustration of talent and a limitation on males of the capacity for nurturance, warmth, tenderness or of excelling in the 'feminine' realms of home baking or knitting. Somehow and probably wrongly, we take such consequences less seriously than a loss of employment potential. Certainly, it is easier to demonstrate loss of potential in careers and occupations than it is in the privatised sphere of the home". The issue of equal opportunities applies then to both boys and girls, and if there is going to be substantial change within the family and the work place, the attitudes of both boys and girls to each other must alter significantly.

An anti-sexist approach in careers education is unlikely to make much impact unless the whole school provides support. This view is embodied in a recent book edited by Janie Whyld (1983). School organisation and control, classroom interaction and the subject curriculum are all seen as combining to show where a school stands in regard to sexist practice. Careers education is merely a part, albeit an important part, of this process, although it could play a key role as a focus for the essential issues of sexism in schools.

At the heart of countering sexism is sex role stereotyping. Bould and Hopson (1983) list a series of examples of this sort of stereotyping observed in schools as part of an EOC research project. The stereotyping extended to all areas of school life, from the school structure with men, predominantly, in senior posts to work experience schemes which mirrored stereotypical "male/female" occupations. It is clear from this list that there is much that can be done that can support initiatives taken within careers education.

Hansen (1974) suggested 7 specific strategies for consideration by those working in careers education.

(1) Awareness of the counsellor's own attitudes, expectations and practices regarding women clients. This will require some external monitoring as much of this is unconscious.

(2) Need to know and help clients obtain accurate information about trends in work and society in general. Many changes in employment patterns, legislation, family structure, etc., have occurred in recent years and counsellors must keep up to date with these and be able to transmit them to their clients.

(3) An awareness of sex bias in careers literature, tests and questionnaires. Despite equal opportunities legislation, this bias is still apparent, and influential.

(4) A need to help young women and men become aware of the options available to them in education, employment, lifestyles and career patterns. The

emphasis is deliberately on women and men as stereotyping applies to both. Careers education should be a mixed activity with girls being exposed to the same experiences as boys.

(5) A need to help girls and boys learn the processes involved in decision making. Here the emphasis is on presenting girls with the view that they do have choices regarding their future and that they can make decisions for themselves.

(6) Provide girls with a variety of role models with whom they can identify and from whom they can learn that multiple roles are possible, desirable and real.

(7) A need to involve parents more systematically and developmentally in the career development process of girls and boys. In a sense, if this does not happen, all other strategies are likely to be hindered.

More recently, the Department of Employment Careers Service Branch (1986) have contributed to the question of how Careers Officers should respond to the issue of equal opportunities. They recommend that each Careers Service should have a policy statement committed to equal opportunities generally - in race, handicap and sex, and that a Careers Officer should be designated to co-ordinate equal opportunities initiatives, although it is the responsibility of all Careers Offices to pursue equal opportunities for girls and boys.

High youth unemployment is not a good context in which to try and initiate changes in occupational entry. Indeed, there is evidence that unemployment and limited opportunities are working against girls breaking away from traditional occupations and attitudes. West and Newton's study (1983) suggested that "females exchange of dependence on parents for dependence on a husband in return for adult status can create frustration and depression after marriage". Whyld (1983) also points to a "new and worrying phenomenon of girls going directly into marriage and motherhood as a 'way out' of the dole queue and the scramble for jobs. Girls are resorting to marriage to confer upon themselves the status which is denied them in the labour market".

At the heart of the question of equal opportunities lies the curriculum. The EOC (1985) identify three non educational factors that "influence the education of 5-16 year olds to the point where the sex of the child is often of greater significance than individual ability or potential". The factors are

(1) the masculine image, which is generally prevalent in society, of science, mathematics and technology.

(2) the male-orientation of teaching materials across the curriculum (with the exception of home economics).

(3) the negative attitude of the peer group.

(4) lack of guidance and counselling at the pre-option stage regarding the consequence of dropping certain subjects.

As regards the last point, the EOC call for "a much stronger statement on behalf of the DES in relation to careers education" and "strongly recommend that careers education should have a place in the core curriculum 11-14 in the secondary schools".

Whyte (1981) concludes that "schools ought to be preparing children for life as it will actually be in the future. It can be argued that traditional careers education has not kept pace with social trends. The changes required demand not so much an input of money or staff or resources, as a change in attitude, a new way of looking at sex differences and a conscientisation or raising of awareness about how schools which reinforce sex stereotyping disadvantage children of both sexes". This constitutes a real challenge to parents, teachers and youngsters, but is essential in order to meet the needs of both girls and boys in the future.

The disadvantages in employment, training and education faced by black youngsters has received increasing prominence. The place of careers education in this debate is discussed at some length by Watts and Law (1985). As with the issue of sexism, racism is a delicate, complex and controversial subject and inevitably, a number of conflicting positions have emerged as to how careers education should be best addressed to the very real problems of black pupils. For instance, is the problem to do with cultural differences, or colour prejudice or with disadvantage in general? Similarly, not all ethnic groups experience the same disadvantage. Watts and Law identify three different groups - those with little hold in the labour market, those who have successfully "colonised" particular sectors of the labour market and those who are successfully "integrating". They go on to suggest that careers education should have one or more of the following underlying aims - to assimilate ethnic minority pupils into the dominant culture; to reinforce their existing culture; to provide access to skills, etc. of dominant culture, whilst valuing their existing culture. With the last aim, there is a very real problem of cultural conflict and a loss of identity. Ultimately, black youngsters are faced with the alternatives of "joining the whites", "opting out", or "playing the system".

Five strategies are suggested by Watts and Law.

(1) To provide compensatory teaching for ethnic minority pupils in employability skills and/or knowledge of the labour market. This makes an assumption of some "cultural deficit", rooting the problem in the black community rather than within the white host society. This strategy, if applied alone, does not deal with the structural problems that lead to disadvantage and discrimination in employment.

(2) To extend the range of "role models" to which ethnic minority youngsters have access. This strategy has been put forward in relation to girls as well and is supported more generally in earlier research by Law (1981).

(3) To extend the range of informal networks to which ethnic-minority youngsters have access. These networks are important in job seeking and evidence suggests that black school leavers are more dependent on formal agencies than are whites. Whether schools can effectively play a part in these informal networks must be questionable because of their "informal" nature.

(4) To prepare ethnic minority pupils to deal with the racial discrimination they may meet in the labour market (and elsewhere). This should include such pupils knowing what their rights are and what for instance, the Careers Service could do in relation to employers suspected of discrimination. The question of bringing this emotive issue into the open for discussion requires sensitivity and skill.

(5) To explore socio-political issues related to the opportunities open to ethnic minorities. As Watts and Law say, there is a tendency for careers education to deal with highly political matters in a very

depoliticised way. Ultimately, it is difficult to achieve balance in such matters, and most teachers are likely to take the safe way out and avoid such issues.

Two final issues are raised. Firstly, if there is a case for some distinctive provision on careers for black youngsters, should this be done with them alone? The same discussion about advantages and disadvantages for "consciousness raising" applies to girls as well. The second issue has to do with white teachers needing opportunities to explore the racism within themselves in order to be more effective in working with ethnic minority pupils. The question of how far white as opposed to black teachers and careers officer can ultimately help such youngsters stems from this.

There has been a substantial national debate about the achievement of black children in our schools, culminating in the publication of the Swann Report in 1985. Its interim report (Rampton 1981) specifically highlighted shortcomings in careers education and advice. The report stated that "West Indians have claimed that low expectations of their children on the part of both careers teachers and careers officers lead to the children being discouraged from aspiring to the full range of post school opportunities available....... Schools need to do far more to prepare their pupils for adult life". The issue of the education and work experiences of 15-18 year olds from ethnic minority groups was explored in depth by a recent DES study (1985). The study shows that the low achievement of black pupils is very frequently a consequence of the social system including the schools rather than something that is inescapable. Eggleston, director of the project observes that whilst "schools and colleges cannot fundamentally change the labour market, nor eradicate structural unemployment, they certainly can enhance the employability of many young people and even develop their entrepreneurial and occupational skills far more fully as well as removing the impediment to achievement in more conventional areas". An imaginative and comprehensive careers education programme should form the basis of any school's effort to put these objectives into practice.

Schools Council Careers Education and Guidance Project

The project was established in 1971 and first

Careers Education Under Pressure

published materials in 1977. It is an important development because it is the only major national curriculum programme in careers education. A wide variety of materials were produced; many of them highly innovative. The project generated an important debate about the philosophy as well as the process of careers education, so that although some of the materials have become "dated", the questions that the project posed are still highly relevant. The materials are designed for 3, 4, 5th year classes. They are described as "flexible" and can be used in separate careers courses or integrated into other subjects. The philosophy behind the project can be identified in various statements made in the introduction to the teachers guides:

(1) - "Ideally it should be an integral part of the whole curriculum for all age groups" (The material is promoted as fitting into the traditional curriculum as well as providing the basis for a careers education programme).

(2) - "There is more to careers education than jobs because there is more to choosing a life after school than just training about jobs".

- "The course helps children to understand more about their relationships with others, the effect they have on people and the effects other people have on their lives".

- "Work is so important in human life that pupils need to understand how work will affect their lives and how through work they can contribute to society and to their own satisfaction as individuals". (Careers Education as part of wider programme of social education concerned with life style, relationships and social skills).

(3) - "So that they can gain an increasing measure of control over their own lives".

- "Any Careers Education programme.... which does not help individuals understand what they can do to control their own lives is of limited value".

- "Lacking confidence to do anything to change themselves or their situation they are soon alienated and exploited; they suffer and society suffers. Careers education is an attempt to help individuals avoid drifting, alienation and exploitation".

- "No one can go through life as a responsible citizen without accepting some responsibility for his own action. People should neither abdicate responsibility for themselves not indiscriminately blame others. The material will have achieved its longterm aim if pupils come to realise that they are responsible for their own actions and that they and society will benefit from the quality of their own understanding, participation and efforts".
(Careers Education as concerned with control, power, personal responsibility).

(4) - "The material reflects a real world which is problematical and provides ways in which pupils can become aware of issues which are already affecting their lives or will do so in the near future".

- "Throughout the course, the basic endeavour is that of facilitating skill in raising questions and then answering them constructively".

- "The basic aim is therefore to help pupils to develop balanced and realistic conceptions of work".
(Careers Education encouraging a questioning and reflective approach to a wide range of work related issues).

Important messages are being transmitted by the project's materials. Clearly, there is a suggestion that young people need to be given confidence to "control their own lives" otherwise they will drift, become alienated and exploited. It is not made clear who will exploit them, although it is fair to assume that this exploitation is likely to take place at work. There is also an assumption that young people are especially vulnerable to external forces that can lead to alienation and exploitation and that they need to be adequately prepared at school to counter these tendencies. However, the term "responsible citizen" is then used to place responsibility firmly on individuals for their actions - and "indiscriminately blaming others" is warned against. On the one hand, the terms alienation and exploitation suggest a Marxist analysis of

101

capitalism, whilst the later statement presents an individualistic or liberal perspective on entry into the labour force, stating that individuals have the means to control their own lives, and to be autonomous, if properly prepared.

There does seem to be some inherent theoretical conflict as regards the underlying aims of the project which is difficult to resolve. This is made harder to deal with in a period of high unemployment where the degree of individual control over "life chances" has been severely reduced. The scope for "alienation" and "exploitation" has become that much greater. The relative lack of emphasis on unemployment could be attributed to the fact that the project work (1971-77) preceded the very rapid and sustained increase in youth unemployment.

Despite this, it is worth examining the material on unemployment more closely. This represents one of eight magazines of 16 pages that constitute "Work" Part 2; the fourth year materials. The magazine's front cover proclaims "Half the population of this country is unemployed", and serves as a basis for introductory discussion. The aim is to "help pupils view unemployment in a wider perspective. It will help them to appreciate that work is not synonymous with paid employment and that for many people the most meaningful part of their lives is carried out outside their official employment".

This aim can certainly be seen as realistic and worth highlighting, although it could be said to avoid the issue of why this is so. It can also be seen as deterministic, and contrary to the philosophy of "taking control of one's life" that underlies many of the statements on the teachers' guides. There are four more detailed objectives listed.

(1) To examine why some people choose not to have a job even though they are able to do one.

(2) To explore why many people are prevented from having a job, even though they want one.

(3) To consider the question "Does everyone have the right to work?"

(4) To decide what people can do to overcome unemployment.

These objectives certainly need to be fully and honestly explored if young people are to understand their predicament now and in the future. The

Careers Education Under Pressure

project's materials may be getting outdated, because of the course of time, but the issues they are addressing are still very live and pertinent.

Two statements outlining different standpoints illustrate the ideological tension that exists in all careers education. The statements, four years apart, arise from the work of the project team.

"Careers Education must enable pupils to understand and evaluate their own society as a work originator and help them to anticipate their own contribution in the future. In an age of technological innovation and international competition which both stimulates and hinders change, pupils will need to develop flexibility and critical judgement. They will be required to respond to changing circumstances, some of which do not always enhance the quality of their lives and they will therefore need to participate in change in such a way that their contribution is both responsibile to the aims of production and to their desires for personal fulfilment. Self knowledge derived through an understanding of the purposes and the conditions of work is a key element in the project's approach to careers education". Work, Part 3, introduction (pub. 1979).

Contrast this with:

"But what about the large group of children for whom choosing between different jobs and their accompanying lifestyles can in reality only make a marginal difference to the quality of life and who, moreover, must struggle harder to develop any genuine self awareness given the concepts of themselves imposed by their environment. For these children the relevance of choosing is less accessible. It is not choosing which will answer the problems they experience at work but changing, changing the conditions of work, changing the society in which they live". (1975 in Bates et al, 1984).

The earlier statement is a great deal more challenging and radical than the statement made four years later. The dramatic shift is probably due to pressure to produce a more "balanced" statement of aims, which would conform more closely to the status quo. The later statement focusses on non-controversial "value-free" factors such as "technological innovation and international competition" as causing change and implies that they are not controllable, certainly not by individuals.

Careers Education Under Pressure

In reality, there are choices as to the acceptability of technological change as Greenpeace has demonstrated, and to the impact of international competition through the options such as import quotas as the Japanese have shown. Change will "not always enhance the quality of their lives" is a bland statement that begs the issue of how unevenly the impact of change falls upon individuals and what the basis for these differences are. The statement is made even more questionable by the expression "responsible to the aims of production and to their desires for personal fulfilment". This implies some personal "balancing act" between the aims of production which in a capitalist economy is predominantly the maximisation of profit and personal fulfilment which could include good pay, autonomy, and good working conditions which are likely to reduce profit levels. There will certainly always be some conflict between these two objectives and the statement fails to indicate how this can be resolved, apart from using the word "responsible", which implies not disturbing the status quo.

Bates et al (1984) pose the questions "What is the working class interest in the world of work?", and answer it as follows.
"Young people are not directly interested in the ´success of industry´ nor in discipline nor in transferable skills nor in flexible working - ´work´ from the employer´s point of view. They want the power of ´skill´ in the market place of jobs, local information and local access to jobs and to the wage".
Self awareness or self knowledge is described as a "key element in the project´s approach to careers education". Whilst not disputing the importance of self awareness, or the significance of identity formation, such concepts have little or no meaning outside the social context in which they exist. For instance, it is hardly possible to understand the self awareness of a black youngster in South Africa without considering apartheid. Equally, it is not feasible to understand the complexities that surround the formation of a girl´s self awareness in Britain today without reference to sex role stereotyping.

Finally, it is worth considering an earlier Schools Council project, on the Humanities which has a section on "People and Work". One of the central project team John Elliott relates the project to the concept of vocational guidance. Elliott (1975) describes vocational guidance as "helping pupils and students to make, in some sense, rational decisions with respect to both the kinds of work they will do, and to the social situations they will encounter at work. These decisions are not merely technical decisions about how best to execute a particular job task or get the job that is wanted, but decisions which often involve controversial social and political values".

Having focussed on the controversial nature of the material, "People and Work" provides a number of organising categories to make up a "map" for pupils to enquire further. These categories include the meaning of work, social stratification and work, obligations and rights in the working situation and conceptions of masculinity and femininity at work. Elliott states that the teacher should attempt to be "procedurally neutral" in handling this material. "In other words, there is a way of exercising positive influence or guidance in socially controversial areas which does not involve using one's authority position as an educator to take sides in favour of one controversial evaluative position rather than another". Unfortunately, the project material does not seem to have had a long lasting impact on schools (Lee, 1984). It does provide a rich range of materials for active learning, which are of direct relevance to careers education, and which could be infused into the curriculum through humanities lessons.

The two Schools Council projects provided the opportunity to radically change the nature of careers education, making it more stimulating, relevant and challenging. This has not happened, and there are a number of likely reasons. Both projects aroused controversy before they were completed. The Humanities project pack on race was withdrawn, and its other materials have come in for regular criticism. The Careers project was the subject of a Schools Council enquiry in 1977. As Bates et al (1984) notes, "one of the main points at issue between the Schools Council and the project was the latter's presentation of industry within its teaching materials". The project was required to present industry in a more "positive" light and this led to a modification in its published materials. Thus both projects were targets for official pressure. Similarly, the material produced by both projects made considerable demands upon existing teaching styles and insufficient training and dissemination led to many schools to not making full use of the opportunities offered by both projects. There seems to have been a lack of enthusiasm amongst many of

105

those in positions of power in education to make this possible.

TRAINING FOR AND APPROACHES TO CAREERS EDUCATION (TRACE)

TRACE is a Schools Council project that looked at the diversity of Careers Education practice (Fawcett, 1985). One of the aspects it examined was the influence of curriculum decisions on the approach to Careers Education adopted in particular schools, and five different approaches emerged.

(1) Subject based curriculum - here careers education appears on the timetable in the same way as other subjects. The advantage of this is that careers "teachers are able to compete for resources and time alongside other colleagues using, as it were, similar currency for bartering". However, "careers education as a subject will be constrained, in ways which may be inappropriate for careers education, e.g. limited or no time for outside visits".

(2) Working across the curriculum - this approach was in considerable evidence in the project schools. It means that more resources can be brought to bear, and competition for status and time is reduced. However, it does require considerable monitoring in case pupils receive a confusing set of perspectives.

(3) The pastoral curriculum - some of the same advantages apply as above. Fawcett does point out that "pastoral systems are, at least in part, disciplinary systems", and that this makes for an uneasy alliance. Similarly, careers education is not suited to "highly protective, parenting approaches to pastoral care".

(4) Resource based curriculum - where the process of learning is emphasised as opposed to the content of the subject. This was influential in a few project schools. It helps pupils acquire "a knowledge and understanding of themselves which is transferable to adult and working life".

(5) An open school approach - the community school offers opportunities for "first hand contact with adult working like, the world for which careers education is supposed to be a preparation". However, what is learnt is much harder to control and may

require "different skills and resourcefulness from teachers".

Fawcett sees all these approaches as having advantages and disadvantages. However, "the most startling differences occur between the intention of the schools and individual teachers on the one hand and the benefit experienced by students on the other. Those who wish to explore this for themselves should look out for cosmetic and compensatory approaches to careers education as well as those based on the curriculum entitlement of individuals students". Fawcett makes a strong plea for a whole school debate about the place of careers education in the curriculum.

In conclusion, she identifies four elements which were regularly discussed by participants in the project. They are

(1) Careers education is about work; the work ethic, paid employment, unemployment, how people occupy their time, housework, alternatives to unemployment, etc. This is a matter for debate between teachers, students, parents and others from outside the school and it is one which has a profound effect on the curriculum either overtly or covertly.

(2) Careers education is about enabling individual growth and development and this calls for specialist expertise in inter-personal skills.

(3) Schools wish to respond to change but do not always know how. It is the task of a careers specialist to monitor change; to interpret possible implications for the curriculum and the future of students; and to communicate all of this to colleagues, to students themselves and to relevant people outside the schools.

(4) Careers education must be concerned with the provision of a wide range of diverse types of information, together with specific teaching and practice of information skills.

TRACE is valuable in a number of respects, not least in that it makes it quite clear that teachers as a whole must consider the issues raised by careers education and must pay close attention to their role in the process of preparing students for adult life.

Careers Education Under Pressure

Conclusion

Much is being demanded of careers education today. On the one hand, the emphasis is on personal development as being intimately linked to careers education which has led commentators such as Best et al (1984) to state that "careers education should be thought of something much wider than guidance into a career or counselling in the face of difficult option choices. It should also facilitate learning about the whole complex structure of relationships within which each individual has to spend a good part of his working life and which more than any other factor may affect the rest of life as well". Whilst on the other hand, the more utilitarian requirements of the MSC are demanding that careers education motivates youngsters to enter occupations that the economy needs filling, despite high levels of youth unemployment in many areas.

Watts (1986) observes that careers education has been "increasingly linked with - and sometimes, subsumed within - three other curriculum trends". Firstly, the pastoral curriculum has integrated careers education into active tutorial work, for example. Secondly, the school-industry links, stimulated by the Schools Council Industry project, have inevitably overlapped with careers education. Finally, particular initiatives like CPVE and TVEI have careers education incorporated into them. One result of these developments has been a relative weakening in the position of careers teachers, according to Watts. There is a danger in this interlinking and subsuming that careers education will lose its "identity" and impact. This could certainly be true if in fact careers teachers are now in a weaker position.

The TRACE project indicated that there is still much to be done in promoting careers education within the school as a whole. A lead at Local Authority and national level is required to rationalise and integrate the diversity of approaches and resources now available. For instance, job ideas and information generator - computer assisted learning (JIIG CAL) is a good example of a system that has grown and developed, whilst being adopted, as a rule, in a piecemeal fashion by Careers Services, and schools. It offers an interesting and important contribution to careers education, but only if it is implemented, with pupils, as planned. Careers education requires time, resources and trained committed staff. It rarely has all these ingredients.

CHAPTER 5

POLITICAL EDUCATION - TOO HOT TO HANDLE?

> "There is no opposition to, or argument for, political education which does not involve a political stance. Opposition to political education must involve anti-democratic ideology. It seeks to define the population of knowledge of political structure and policy and thus represents an obstacle to informed democratic political debate". (Demaine, 1981).

It is estimated that nearly one third of all new voters did not vote in the 1983 General Election, whilst as many as 47% of 18-22 year olds who were unemployed did not vote at this Election. (Crewe, 1983). These findings are borne out in a large survey of teenagers. (DES, 1983). It showed that three quarters acknowledged that they were politically apathetic. However, they did feel strongly "that there was a lack of opportunity to make themselves heard in the adult world both through lack of understanding on the part of adults and their views, if expressed, being generally ignored". Again, it is significant that unemployed teenagers in particular felt disenfranchised, especially as far as being ignored was concerned. An earlier survey by Stradling (1977) had also demonstrated low levels of political knowledge amongst school leavers. However, three quarters of this group did agree that they ought to know more about current affairs and politics; and nearly half said that they were very or fairly interested in politics. All these findings indicate a need for better political education in schools.

Political Education - Too Hot to Handle?

What is Political Education?

What is meant by political education needs to be explored and clarified. Gillespie (1981) defines political education as "the development of competencies in thinking about and acting in political arenas". She explores this further by identifying four approaches. Firstly, values have always been central to political matters and is concerned with "commitments and loyalties to groups, to nations or to the global political system as part and parcel of a discussion of political education", but also more widely to a concern for justice and moral education. Secondly, information about political institutions, issues and personalities is clearly of key importance. It can be seen as quite different from the first approach but as essentially linked to it. Thirdly, inquiry can be seen as central to political education. Using this approach, students can be encouraged to clarify ideas and values, as well as become more effectively involved in the political process. Fourthly, participation can be regarded as the essential means by which students learn. The school can be seen as a "laboratory for citizenship instruction and the goals are not so much to solve the problems in the school or community, but to provide appropriate transfer experiences for the skills students are learning". Gillespie concludes by saying that "change, complexity and respect for human dignity are equally important ideas".

In comparison with other Western countries, political education has been slow to emerge as part of the curriculum. Whitty (1985) accounts for this in terms of England's "liberal humanist conceptions of culture" and he sees "a relatively stable society, has favoured implicit means of socialisation into status quo and has thus been much less overtly obsessed with the need to inculcate pupils with its dominant ideology than societies experiencing rapid social change or trying to legitimate a new political regime". A number of factors can account for the advent of political education, such as the lowering of the voting age to 18, a concern for political apathy amongst youngsters and a growing support for the National Front among others, as well as mounting evidence of widespread political ignorance.

Just how much political education there is within schools today is difficult to estimate. The Curriculum Review Unit conducted a survey which showed that 79% of all middle and secondary schools in England and Wales claim to be providing some

Political Education - Too Hot to Handle?

political education, although, in many cases, a modest provision through subjects such as history and general studies (Stradling and Norton, 1983). This inevitably reflects a considerable diversity of provision, which Porter (1982) regards as due to lack of planning. He goes on to add that political education may be unique in being both high risk, because of its controversial subject matter and low status, because it is not an examination subject.

The impact of political education is, by its very nature difficult to evaluate. Stradling (1977) quotes evidence from a number of countries where it is a well established feature of the curriculum that suggests there has been little impact on students' political attitudes, knowledge or behaviour. Mercer (1974) investigated a modern studies course in Scotland and came to the conclusion that "to ring in a new and essentially contrived agent and assume that wholesale transformations in political education will occur is quite unrealistic".

Stradling (1977) came to the conclusion that "there is something essentially paradoxical about a democracy in which 80-90% of future citizens (and the present citizenry) are insufficiently well informed about local, national and international policies to know not only what is happening but also how they are affected by it and what they can do about it. Most of the political knowledge which they do have is of a rather inert and voyeuristic kind and of little use to them either as political consumers or as political actors". In recent years, much has been made of low standards of achievement in subjects such as mathematics, but little or no popular attention has been given to political illiteracy.

As Hargreaves (1982) points out, "Politicians tend to be suspicious of party politics in schools, and yet they also expect the schools to educate young people to take a genuine interest in politics at national and local levels and to play active roles as participants in democratic society. They bewail the widespread ignorance and apathy concerning political life and yet refuse to let schools do the work that is essential to making improvements in the commitments of the young in the political arena...... The truth is that political cynicism among people will persist until we give political education more attention and until politicians themselves show more willingness to be accountable". There is a clear double message to schools in what Hargreaves observes to be happening in the political arena.

If political education is seen as "preparation

111

Political Education - Too Hot to Handle?

for citizenship", this has been an acceptable concept in the secondary curriculum for many years and a more generalised objective since the 1870 Education Act. Whitty (1985) comments that this "rather passive concept of education for citizenship, in the form of civics and similar courses, was a significant feature of the curriculum of the secondary modern schools". Such courses could accurately be described as essentially instruction in obedience and social adjustment rather than genuine political education.

It is interesting to note that the Swann Report (1985) identified political education as having the potential to lay "the foundations of a genuinely pluralist society and countering the influence of racism". The report advocates an active approach in line with the "Programme for Political Education" and encourages a critical awareness amongst pupils. The argument that pupils are not mature enough to deal with sensitive issues like racism is not accepted. Indeed, the report maintains that political education "can be especially important in relation to pupils of ethnic minority origin where families may be unfamiliar with the institutions and procedures which exist in this country". Lord Scarman is quoted as saying "righty or wrongly, young black people do not feel politically secure, any more than they feel economically or socially secure".

The apparent trend towards political education in schools has brought about a counter attack from the "New Right". Parkins (1986) presents a series of arguments against the provision of political education in schools. These centre around the contention that the subject is not a suitable one for young people whilst at school and also that it is open to bias, especially from the left. He portrays Marxists as using political education and "threatening the continuance of normal democratic politics". Scruton (1986) describes peace studies in the same way, relegating it to postgraduate level. Indeed, the "New Right" is suspicious of any sort of social science teaching in schools. Regan (1986) attacks sociology and politics teaching in schools as being intellectually too demanding and also open to bias, which is sometimes deliberate. Their concerted attacks illustrate the struggle that is taking place over political education, not just within education but in the political arena as well.

Political Education - Too Hot to Handle?

Guidance and counselling in the context of political education

There can be no doubt that political education has evoked some of the most heated debate surrounding the curriculum in recent years. In one sense this is hardly surprising because of the widely held view that education should be apolitical. However, the debate, often muddled though it may be, does illustrate some much more profound areas of conflict which are fundamental to the very nature of British education. The issues surround the limits of the curriculum, the role of teachers, and the role and status of schools within wider society. At the level of the pupil, the debate about political education calls into question the future role, power and involvement of the next generation in the political process. Yet even more widely than this, political education is about each individual's quest for self fulfilment, autonomy, equal participation within society and their wider responsibility as citizens. Seen in this context, it should form an integral part of the pastoral curriculum, and in the pupil's quest for self development.

If we accept Shertzer and Stone's (1981) definition of guidance as "the process of helping individuals to understand themselves and their world" political education must form an important part of a programme of guidance within the school. It is also interesting to see how one of the key figures in the counselling movement, Carl Rogers, in recent years has focussed attention on the notion of "personal power". He describes the politics of the traditional school as based on seven principles:

- the teacher as the possessor of knowledge, the student a recipient.

- the lesson as the means of pouring knowledge into the student and the examination as the measure of the extent to which he has received it.

- the teacher as the possessor of power, the student the one who obeys.

- authoritarian rule is the accepted policy in the classroom.

- trust is at a minimum.

- the students are best controlled by being kept

Political Education - Too Hot to Handle?

in an intermittent or constant state of fear.

- there is no place for the whole person in the education system, only for the intellect.

Rogers (1985) offers an alternative person-centred learning which has clear links to personal and social education. It is based on the teacher as a facilitator, who shares the responsibility for learning with others - the students, parents and the community. The student develops his own programme of teaching, with an emphasis on self discipline and self evaluation. In Rogers's words "the political implications of person-centred education are clear: the student retains his own power and control over himself; he shares in the responsible choices and decisions; the facilitator provides the climate for these aims". Rogers is writing about radical changes to the whole nature of schooling, some of which can be seen in recent proposals (White, Brockington and Pring, 1985) and actual initiatives, for example, CPVE. However, the thrust of what he is proposing has direct relevance to the subject matter of political education. It also makes direct links between the objectives of the pastoral curriculum, which by definition should be person centred, and the rest of the curriculum.

Where does political education belong?

The issue of where political education belongs in the curriculum is problematic. Outside "Politics and Government" courses there are clear links with history, social studies and economics, and it is within these disciplines that much "political education" is claimed to be taught. However, these are only subjects likely to deal with the more factual aspects of political education, and it is the teaching process that is as important as the content. In this sense, political education can be seen to belong more readily within a personal and social education programme. As the CRU report points out "Although politics may (or may not) form a discrete part of a social programme, social education by virtue of the fact that it deals in part with relationships between individuals and society, must have a political dimension. The political dimension is manifest not only in the concerns of explicit social education programmes but also in the content of other areas of the curriculum and in the methods and styles of teaching employed in the classroom. Political learning may be influenced by characteristics of the management and organisation of a school as well as by the general ´climate´ or ´ethos´ of personal relationships". (CRU, 1983).

Establishing a place and identity for political education has been a problem, as has its "boundaries". For instance, does political education include third world, peace and women´s studies? Is political education really the same as moral education? The current uneasy position occupied by political education can only be understood by examining the history of social and political education during the last 40 years (Whitty, 1985). Whitty sees three specific attempts to change the nature of social and political education during this time. In the first instance the social studies movement incorporated social education into the "pastoral" rather than "academic" provision of many schools which served to reinforce its low status. Subsequently, the new social studies served to establish sociology and a sociology based social studies as a subject like any other in the school curriculum.

The third movement has been particularly associated with the Politics Association and the Hansard Society´s programme for political education. It sought to move away from the over-academic approach to politics represented in most GCE syllabuses. In the programme first discussion document, the aims and objectives were outlined as folows. "We want to get away from the idea of a ´politics syllabus´ which is a progressive simplification of a University discipline. Rather we plan to build from bottom up by examining early perceptions of politics in non-academic contexts and streams, and to elaborate a growing process of political literacy through whatever discipline (in most of which the influence of political science on the teacher is obviously only a very small factor)".

The Programme for Political Education

In 1974 the Hansard Society for Parliamentary Government in collaboration with the Politics Association obtained a grant from the Nuffield Foundation to develop a political education curriculum. The programme was intended to focus upon a form of political education relevant to the real world in which pupils live. In doing this, Crick and

Political Education - Too Hot to Handle?

Porter (1978) coined the term "political literacy" involving "the knowledge, skills and attitudes needed to make a person informed about politics, able to participate in public life of all kinds and to recognise and tolerate diversities of political and social values". There was a deliberate attempt to get away from an over-academic approach as represented by most existing examination syllabuses on the subject.
The political literacy approach is based upon four main features.

(1) A very broad conception of politics referring to group behaviour at school and everyday life as well as to the activities of political parties and pressure groups.

(2) Political issues form the focus of teaching and are used to consider what should be done, why, how and when people disagree.

(3) An emphasis on the developments of a conceptual framework for understudy political activities and behaviour.

(4) Emphasis on acquiring practical knowledge and politically relevant skills.

Crick and Lister (1978) produced a specification for teaching political literacy in the classroom, which is represented in diagram 1.
Stradling (1984) described the programme's curriculum strategy as a combination of claiming a slot for political education on the timetable and of infiltrating it through other subjects. In Crick and Porter's words (1978) "the frontal attack was to be a generalised programme or outline for local adaptation as a two year course and the permeation was a strategy of infusing political literacy into the curriculum through other subject disciplines". Thus a series of guidelines for curriculum development were established, whilst groups of teachers were formed to produce draft syllabuses incorporating the guidelines with different subject areas. Stradling comments that "the project encountered its fair share of problems and failures". Certainly, the infusion approach runs the danger of producing political literacy that is greatly watered down. Teachers who are not specialists in the subject are likely to fall back and "concentrate more on the transmission of knowledge rather than the development of skills and conceptual understanding".

Diagram 1

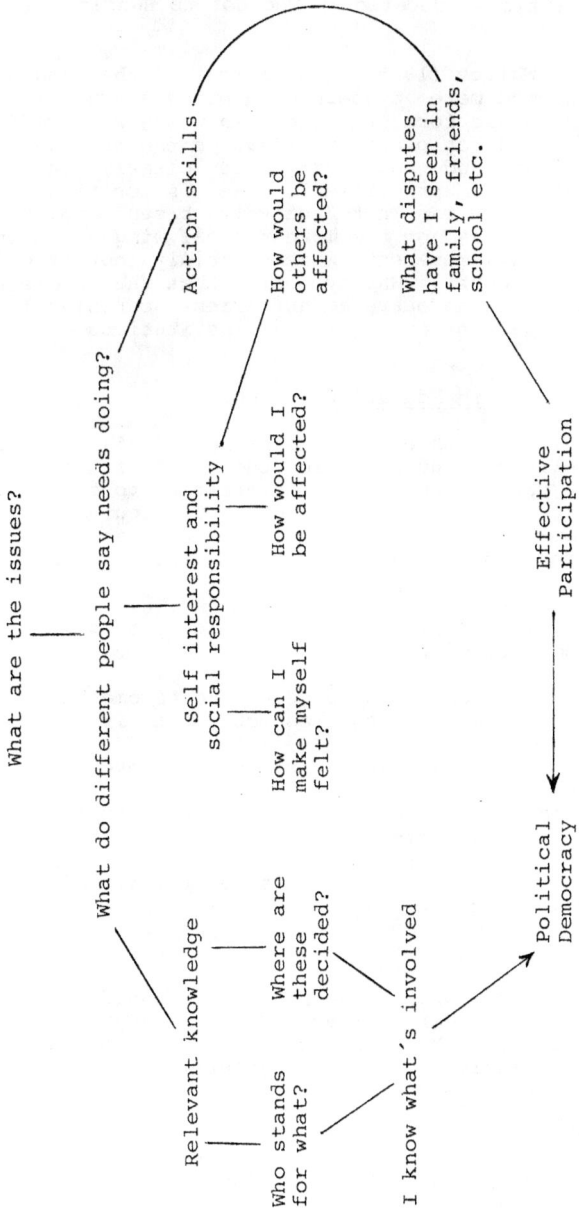

Political Education - Too Hot to Handle?

Whitty (1985) is critical of the programme as it "seemed more concerned to preserve than improve upon the basic form of society in which we lived" and this "helped to place its ideas on the national political agenda and made it more clearly in line with "national priorities". He is critical that the programme was not "actively based" enough and that the "ideas of the more radical wing of the political literacy movement were certainly not in evidence in the report". Whitty feels that the whole programme did not advocate a sufficient searching look at the adequacy of our political institutions.

The Law in Education Project

White, Brockington and Pring (1985) link legal to political and economic studies as part of a "new" 14-18 curriculum. It is interesting to observe that the Law Society and School Curriculum Development Committee have recently established a "Law in Education" project (L.E.P.). The project sets out four aims for pupils.

(1) To enable young people to gain a better understanding of law.

(2) To enable young people to become better informed about relevant legal aspects of their lives.

(3) To enable young people to develop linguistic, decision making and problem-solving skills which enhance their ability to behave appropriately in law-related matters.

(4) To encourage an attitude of independence and self confidence in law-related matters whilst remaining open minded and respectful of the reasonably held views of others.

The links between this project and political education are clear. For instance, key concepts identified by the project such as (a) many laws seek to resolve or limit conflict, (b) laws can be instruments of social policy, and (c) many laws are influenced in their formation by sectional interests have obvious overlap with political education. Similarly, the skills of reasoning, enquiry and interpersonal skills listed by the project are closely related to those outlined earlier in this chapter by Gillespie (1981) in describing political education. Finally, the project states that "the law touches on many issues of controversial or political nature where differing views are sincerely held by reasonable members of society. It is important, therefore, that young people be encouraged to recognise this fact and to think through their own ideas on appropriate matters and to be able to hold them and defend them with reasoned argument". This aim is one that would be endorsed by many of those engaged in political education.

Certificate of Pre-vocational Education

The Certificate of Pre-Vocational Education (CPVE) has ten areas which make up its core, and two of these make specific reference to political education. Firstly, personal and career development includes an aim "to consider a range of social, moral and ethical issues and formulate personal values by recognising the relationship between rights and responsibilities of citizens in a democratic society". Secondly, industrial, social and environmental studies aims "to develop awareness of political considerations in order to understand and participate in the social environment by:

(1) participating in a variety of decision making activities and evaluating the methods by which decisions are reached.

(2) identifying the individual's rights and opportunities for political involvement and the factors upon which these depend.

(3) investigating and explaining common features of political processes in a range of contexts.

(4) investigating the differences between the major British political parties.

(5) explaining the roles and responsibilities of local and central government and the effects of their activities.

(6) identifying and explaining the purposes of the major international political and economic organisations.

These elements between them constitute a substantial element of political education and

Political Education - Too Hot to Handle?

represent a significant step towards making political education part of the core curriculum, albeit at post 16. It is too early to evaluate how far these elements will be taught in practice or how they will be approached.

Political Education as Part of Personal and Social Education

Making political education an effective part of the curriculum is clearly beset with many problems. These problems present a strong case for integrating it into programmes of PSE. The educational arguments for this approach are twofold. Firstly, the content of a political education programme has clear links with PSE, and secondly, and more importantly, the process of teaching both types of programme are the same. As Stradling (1981) points out, "teachers (of PE) cannot rely solely on directive teaching or "chalk and talk", but need to be skilled in organising group exercises, projects, games and simulations and in enabling enquiry based learning to flourish". The "political" arguments for integration rest on the assumption that political education is more acceptable (and less visible) within a broad developmental programme that attempts to deal with the whole person.

Pring (1984) maps the "territory" of the formal curriculum for personal and social development. He locates political education within social studies and identifies three specific applications; citizenship/ membership of the state, community participation and the role of law. He sees "personal development.... as gradually taking on responsibility for one´s own decisions as well as respecting the ability of others to establish their own priorities". Political education can provide an understanding that should be at the centre of the curriculum "for without them the democratic ideals we value are in danger of being subverted - from the extreme right as well as from the extreme left". This view was supported by the HMI paper on "political competence" (DES 1977) which also envisaged the "pastoral curriculum" as playing an important role in political education.

Having made a case for political education being a part of a wider personal and social education programme, it is instructive to consider the "political" content of some of the better known programmes. The active tutorial work (ATW) programmes offer teachers tutorial topics for the full secondary

Political Education - Too Hot to Handle?

age range. A high proportion of LEA's are aware of ATW and encourage its use in schools and colleges (Bolam and Medlock, 1985). The fifth year ATW book (1981) sets a number of political objectives for pupils. For instance, "to develop skills in political awareness by examining public income and expenditure". Related activities are "finding out who are the faceless people who make decisions on local affairs", then looking at the sorts of political decisions made locally and considering the issue of priorities. The emphasis is upon action, so the agenda includes organising a petition, writing to local councillors, knowing when and how to vote.

During the second term, pupils objectives include "to develop skills in political awareness: Trade Unions". The issue of joining a Union is considered in the context of questions like "who decides how much I'm paid?" Conflict at work and strikes are examined, whilst it is suggested that a trade unionist, employer and a parent are asked into school to lead discussion. ATW is available for the 16-19 age group as well (1983). There is a substantial amount of material related to political education. Some student objectives are more general; for example, "to develop a critical approach to news, information and opinion". Others are more specific; "to appreciate the concerns of others in the community and to develop an insight into the responsibilities and decision-making of those in charge of community problems". Again the emphasis is upon action, e.g. "How can people organise to put a jointly held point of view?" Students are given assignments and visitors are to be invited in.

The Life Skills Teaching Programmes (Hopson and Scally, 1981, 1982, 1986) have become widely known. "How to develop and use my political awareness" is one of the many lifeskills listed in the programme. None of the programmes deal specifically with political education, although some elements are more generally related to the aims of political education, i.e. "how to be assertive". Similarly, the important work of Leslie Button (1983) which influenced the ATW project, does not deal specifically with political issues but does prepare pupils for their roles in the community, which must include the political.

Stradling (1981) identifies the development of appropriate teacher training courses in political education as crucial to its effective development within schools. He feels that "it is training in the teaching of this subject area which is ignored and yet this is precisely what is most needed in the case of political education. The concern should be less with training subject specialists and more with producing flexible and versatile teachers". The Curriculum Review Unit (1983) have produced a report on teaching political literacy within teacher training. It is interesting to note that it was felt that all student teachers should be alerted to their involvement in and responsibility for the processes of political education. This was in addition to, where possible, institutions offering a professional course option designed to provide a training in the principles and methods of teaching political education. (In 1979, only seven institutions were doing this). It is hard to envisage political education being taught in the imaginative way in which the programme for political education advocated unless there is a firm base within teacher training, and it is unrealistic to expect this to be a priority in in-service training.

At a time when cuts in Higher Education continue to reduce the work of teacher education, the likelihood of developing a "new" subject such as political education seems remote. Political education has much more chance of being treated seriously as part of in-service training for the "pastoral" curriculum. It can be seen as a "life skill" that has a place alongside health, careers, and moral education. The concern for the individual's political rights and responsibilities are all part of a wider preparation for adulthood that most tutors and social educators are intimately involved with and committed to.

The Role of DES and HMI

There has been an HMI working party on Political Education since 1977, and it is important to consider its role as well as more general statements made on this subject by the DES. Two HMI's (Slater and Hennessey) produced a paper on "Political competence" as part of some working papers (DES 1977) which makes some important points. They observe that political education is present in many subjects already and that there is not necessarily a case for a new subject in the curriculum. Beck (1978) is critical of this stance, making the point that political education "cannot be accomplished within the boundaries of 'school subjects'. It requires a much more rigourous and systematic introduction to certain elements of the social sciences than that restriction

Political Education - Too Hot to Handle?

would permit".
Slater and Hennessy do however make a more general observation about the political nature of schooling. They state that "schools are themselves political institutions in that they involve power and authority, participation and the resolution of different options. Children's perceptions of these are arguably a strong influence in the development of their political attitudes". They go on to say that "the pedagogy employed throughout the school has political implications. For example, do we train young people to live in a democracy by talking to them excessively rather than inviting their views? Does repeating copying from textbooks on worksheets produce autonomous citizens?" These are very pertinent questions to the broader issue of political education in the school and illustrates why this area of the curriculum is potentially explosive, and has been slow to develop.

The working paper has a lot to say on attitudes. Toleration, compromise and open mindedness are stressed as essential attitudes in a democracy. However, universal toleration is not prescribed and specifically racism, suppression of opinion, and exploitation of the defenceless are selected as unacceptable. This "middle of the road" liberal stance is further demonstrated in the discussion of skills. Here "the ability to find evidence and evaluate it, to identify slanted interpretation and bias and the ability to understand the predicaments and points of view of others" are picked at as necessary skills. It is striking that there is no mention of developing the skill to take action or to be assertive without which political competence is likely to be distinctly passive. As Porter (1982) observes "political literacy would be limited to a solitary intellectual exercise; the politically literate person would merely be capable of well informed observation and analysis. The ultimate test of effective political education lies in creating a proclivity to action".

Other working papers by HMI's (DES 1977) were more cautious in considering the underlying issues of political education. The paper "Schools and Society" recognise the possible tension between the "socialisation element of education" and the "responsibility for educating the autonomous citizen". It seems that this tension should be resolved in favour of unity and that radical change is not , to be considered. This caution has more recently been expressed in "Better Schools"

Political Education - Too Hot to Handle?

(DES, 1985). Here, the Government's opposition to peace studies is expressed, dismissing it by saying that "the issue of war and peace......naturally arises from many aspects of the curriculum and should be treated in the context in which it arises".

More recently, Slater in School's Council (1984) has restated his position as Chairman of the HMI Working Party on Political Education. In general terms, political education must involve "a consideration of ways in which differences of opinion are resolved in communities, schools, trade unions, youth clubs and perhaps families, and it was even more concerned with the issues than with the machinery for resolution", as well as "an understanding of the machinery of government". Slater feels that many LEAs have moved in this direction, but that there has been a growth in opposition to political education. This opposition comes from various quarters. He also expressed concern at the MSC's antipathy to political education.

Slater however does see political education as potentially having ministerial backing because it deals with the "nature of contemporary society". He identifies seven important areas in particular: the nature of urban society, the role of science and technology, multicultural society, the role of women, patterns of employment and unemployment, the international role of this country and the pluralist nature of our society. In Slater's words, political education is concerned with balance, yet political educators should not claim that political education is free of value judgements. He feels that "too many people in political education believed they were in the business of changing attitudes". This was too ambitious; teachers should aim to "reduce misunderstanding" and inject "nagging grains of doubt".

Conclusion

Before espousing the case for political education too readily, it is as well to take note of Beck's comments (1978). He cautions that "social and political education have too often been banners beneath which profoundly anti-educational activities have flourished and in the present circumstances there is obviously a danger that an officially sponsored programme of political education might turn out to be little more than an attempt to adjust the aspirations of young people to 'realistic' levels and

Political Education - Too Hot to Handle?

to instil 'appropriate' and 'responsible' (i.e. uncritical) attitudes to the world of work". In a period of mass youth unemployment and inner city riots, this temptation must remain great.

Despite the alarm expressed by the new right (O'Keefe, 1986) there is little evidence to suggest that political education is challenging the status quo. As Whitty (1985) puts it, "despite the existence of a small radical wing to the political education movement, its political thrust was very much in line with the expressed priorities of powerful political forces seeking to influence the educational system in the 'national interest'". The varying fortunes of the political education movement can be mirrored by those of the counselling movement. Graham (1986) makes a clear connection between the decline in the number of school counsellors and the discontinuation of counselling courses and the reactionary and conservative swing in the political "pendulum" in the late seventies.

Political education is always likely to be a source of controversy within schools. Indeed, if it ceases to be, it is likely that it is not being taught properly! Stradling (1984) examines the question of teaching controversial issues in general. He points out that controversy exists in all subjects but that some subjects are more sensitive as they deal with contemporary matters. Three concepts are central to this sort of subject matter: balance, neutrality and commitment. Stradling asks whether balance should include the National Front and the Communist Party as well as the major parties.

The concept of neutrality has been closely associated with the Humanities Curriculum Project (HCP); a project with much political education within it. The HCP advocated the teacher's role as that of an impartial chairman of discussion groups, avoiding the assertion of his or her preferences. Commitment relates to teachers making it very clear where they stand on issues, especially if challenged by pupils. This is clearly necessary on occasions when issues like racism or drugtaking may be being discussed.

It is worth considering the history of the HCP as a forerunner of political education. Established in 1967, the project's philosophy embodied much of the thinking behind more recent political education initiatives. Firstly, it was based on the promise that controversial issues should be handled in the classroom by adolescents. The teacher needed to accept a neutral role in not providing his own view. Discussion rather than instruction was to be the

Political Education - Too Hot to Handle?

teaching style, and this should protect differences in view rather than aim for consensus. Finally, the teacher was to act as chairman, responsible for the quality and standards of learning. The project materials focus on social issues, together with social institutions, structures and organisation making for the broad political emphasis advocated by the programme for political education. Much of the material aroused predictable attack from the right, and the Race materials were not actually published.

Lee (1984) states that "the current status of the materials is hard to assess", but she suggests that they are still used but in an isolated way, and not as originally conceived. Her enquiries, however, do suggest that the HCP has made a significant contribution to teaching styles and to how teachers think about the nature of their authority. Important though this is, it does reflect the difficulty that both controversial matter and controversial pedagogic styles have in being accepted and making a significant impact in schools. The HCP was a major attempt to make radical change in the curriculum, and despite its substantial funding and the length of time it was in existence, it seems to have failed in its objectives. This says much for the inertia and inherent conservatism of our schooling and is not encouraging when considering the future of political education.

As so often in education, it is worth returning to Dewey (1916). In exploring the relationship between democracy and education, he saw the individual develop his beliefs and values through participation in social life, and that criticism, questioning and fresh perspectives were essential to a healthy democracy. Likewise, Raymond Williams (1961) makes a powerful plea for a common curriculum that would overcome a situation which "leaves any large number of people at a level of general knowledge and culture below that required by a participating democracy". Prominent in this curriculum is "general knowledge of ourselves and our environment, taught at secondary stage not as separate disciplines but as general knowledge drawn from the disciplines which clarify at a higher stage, i.e. biology, psychology, social history, law and political institutions, sociology, descriptive economics, geography, physics and chemistry". Williams also adds "extensive practice in democratic procedures, including meetings, negotiations and the selection and conduct of leaders in democratic organisations".

Political Education - Too Hot to Handle?

Whitty (1985) feels the way ahead may be with "community studies and humanities programmes that link the development of critical understanding and the fostering of action skills". Whatever the answer, there is no doubt that the issues that surround political education are critical to the healthy development of our nation. As Williams (1961) put it, "it is a question of whether we can grasp the real nature of our society, or whether we persist in social and educational patterns based on a limited ruling class, a middle professional class, a large operative class, cemented by forces that cannot be challenged and will not be changed. The privileges and barriers, of an imported kind, will in any case go down. It is only a question of whether we replace them by the free play of the market or by a public education designed to express and create the values of an education democracy and a common culture".

CHAPTER 6

MANAGING CHANGE: TWO CASE STUDIES

Developments in the area of the pastoral curriculum and within that the more widespread planning of tutorial work has had implications for both the management of change and for in-service training. Programmes which expect teachers to take greater responsibility for the personal and social development of their pupils, in addition to a more traditional welfare function, have inevitably meant that greater demands have been made upon them. The increasing use of activity-based methods in personal and social education programmes has offered teachers a wider repertoire of techniques for teaching, but it has also been a threat for many who may feel that advocates of such methods are, by implication, criticising what has gone on before. For teachers to take on such programmes they need to be convinced of their rationale and of their own ability to deliver them effectively. This chapter will look at two case studies of support for curriculum change in personal and social education, one from a Local Education Authority viewpoint and the other from that of an individual school.

The Berkshire Pastoral Support Team: a local authority initiative

The Berkshire Pastoral Support Team is a group of around twenty full-time teachers, chaired by the county Co-ordinator for Personal and Social Education, which has responsibility for supporting the development of pastoral work in Berkshire. The team meets regularly as a whole group but members also meet and organise courses on a regional basis, a steering committee ensuring that these activities are co-ordinated.

Managing Change: Two Case Studies

The formation of the team came about as a result of the strategy evolved for the dissemination of the Active Tutorial Work Project. Studies such as those of Havelock (1969) had revealed the inadequacies of what he called the "research, development and diffusion" model of curriculum innovation. Most of the Nuffield and Schools Council projects used this strategy, which involved a project team planning, usually on a massive scale over a long period of time, and producing, at high cost, a pack of materials for a more or less passive but rational consumer, who will accept and adopt the innovation if it is offered at the right time and in the right form. This model put the innovating project team at the front of the process and the passive consumers in school at the back. Teachers consequently had no "ownership" of the projects, and once the project teams had left the innovations began to lose their impetus.

The strategy used by the Active Tutorial Work Project Team was, however, much closer to Havelock´s "problem-solving" model which stresses that:-

1. User need is the paramount consideration.

2. Diagnoses of need has to be an integral part of the change process.

3. The outside agent should be non-directive.

4. Internal resources should always be fully utilised.

5. Self-initiated innovation will have the best chance of survival.

In this model the teachers themselves become the agents of change and can use the original project as a springboard for further development long after the original project has ended. It was along these lines that the Berkshire Pastoral Support Team (B.P.S.T) developed.

Team formation

Two of the original members of the team were first recruited by the then Adviser for Personal and Social Education in Berkshire after an initial course run, in 1980, by Jill Baldwin at Maidenhead Teachers´ Centre. These two had an important part to play in

Managing Change: Two Case Studies

the next stage as they helped with the tutoring for another initial course in Reading in February 1981. This course, led by Jill Baldwin and Andy Smith, lasted for two days, with a follow-up day some months later. By the follow-up day course members were expected to have used some of the materials and techniques so that they could report back. Most of the techniques were new to the course members and it was with some trepidation that they were tried out on pupils. It came as a pleasant surprise to many of them that the pupil response was so good and it became clear to many that there was a potential for using the methods in their subject teaching as well as in tutorial work. At the follow-up session the new Adviser for PSE, Anne Gray, was, unbeknown to the course members, "talent spotting" for potential trainees. Six were invited to attend a course in November 1981 to become trainers. Their only commitment was, they were told, to run one six-session course at a teachers' centre afterwards as part of the training. Course members on this residential course came from Sussex, Hampshire, the Isle of Wight, Kent and Guernsey as well as Berkshire and, again led by Jill Baldwin and Andy Smith, the course proved to be the catalyst which eventually led to the formation of the B.P.S.T.

Apart from the wide range of activities, deepening members' experience of the work, and the fruitful cross-county exchanges of experience, the focal point of the course came when course members went, in pairs, into local schools to conduct introductory seminars for staff. This was a totally new experience for the teachers concerned and many still remember the knocking knees, the profound nervousness felt before entering the staff room, the gratitude felt when the staff smiled welcomingly at them and the great sense of elation with which they left after what had been an apparently successful seminar. The importance of such successful field work in this kind of training cannot be over-emphasised.

Developments

The eight trainers were now grouped in pairs, usually male/female, and they organised and tutored four six-session courses in different parts of the county early in 1982. The partnerships had been formed on the residential course and it was made geographically easy for partners to meet to plan the courses. At the same time the close ties formed as a team helped to provide a support group for the various pairs. The courses run were "Active Tutorial Work" courses, run on much the same lines as course members had experienced themselves. As with all courses of this kind the tutors found that they were learning as much as the course members and it became clear that developmental group work approaches had a profound effect on the teacher as well as the taught.

After the success of these courses, the team took on other initial courses and seminars, some at teachers' centres, some within schools after school, some with entire staffs of schools with the schools closed for the day/afternoon, some in teacher training institutions, and some involving Saturdays. The original pairs still tended to work together, although occasionally there would be variations. It was at this stage that one pair was involved with an evaluation of one of their courses, the evaluation being done by a training college lecturer. This had the dual effect of making them think more deeply about their objectives and giving them a greater interest in evaluation; soon after this the lecturer joined the group.

By the time the team had a further residential course in late 1982, it had become apparent that:

(a) More members were needed because of increasing work.

(b) There had been some movement away from the "Active Tutorial Work Project" as such to a more wide ranging interest in personal and social education.

(c) Strategies were needed to ensure that effective teams of tutors were developed in schools.

(d) The group needed to organise itself into a properly recognised team with a chairman and secretary to minute meetings.

It was at this stage that the Berkshire Pastoral Support Team came into being. The aims were numerous but at the forefront was that of promoting and fostering the development of pastoral and tutorial work in Berkshire by taking the initiative in running courses and responding to the expressed needs of schools.

With the help of two members of the national team more members were recruited and trained. Two important points are to be noted here. One was that

Managing Change: Two Case Studies

the trained trainers were now being used to help recruit and train other trainers - the potential was now there for the group to be independent of the national project. The other was that there was the difficulty of assimilating the "old" with the "new" members, a task which required some sensitivity and took some time to complete.

Tutor team courses

It was the next set of courses which helped to weld the team together. A series of courses were run throughout the county on "Effective Tutoring". It was decided to concentrate on tutors of first formers and an invitation was sent to all secondary schools in Berkshire to send their first year team, with their Year Head, to sessions in different parts of the county. The sessions were intensive, hot (in the summer of 1983) and long (2.00-7.00 p.m.) but the response was encouraging. During the afternoon the school groups were allowed to meet on their own to discuss approaches to tutorial work, something which plainly many of the teams had never had the opportunity (or interest) to do before. The success of these sessions encouraged the team to organise similar sessions for the tutors of other year groups in the summer of 1984, but industrial action meant their postponement.

Other activities which team members have been involved in are tutoring on courses outside the county, helping on other in-service courses within the area, running sessions for Deputy Heads with responsibility for Pastoral Work and for Heads of Sixth Form, and helping to run workshops in the N.A.P.C.E. Centre-South region. Sub-groups from within the whole group have met to consider and report back on topics related to the group's work and this has helped stimulate interest in evaluation, racism and pastoral care, and active learning across the curriculum. The regionalisation of the team into three areas, each with a co-ordinator, facilitated the appointment of individual members to take responsibility for liaising with individual schools, thus ensuring more personal contact between the team and schools.

Inevitably team membership has changed as promotions and other responsibilities have meant members leaving. Since much of the work is done outside school hours, the period of industrial action considerably reduced the amount of work for the team,

Managing Change: Two Case Studies

and it said much for the commitment of its members that it kept going. It also says something for the strength of the original idea of creating an independent team, capable of training its own members and organising itself, with county support.

The future

Despite the successful launching of the B.P.S.T. and the amount of work that has been done, it would be wrong to say that all schools in Berkshire are carrying out a programme of tutorial work or personal and social education using the kind of group work techniques advocated in the A.T.W. project. Schools are autonomous in many ways and the team cannot force its way into them; it can only respond to requests after it has made clear what it has to offer. Neither is it easy to follow up and help schools to implement any changes after a course which B.P.S.T. members have run. All members are busy full-time teachers and while this gives them some credibility in running courses, it does, of course, mean that their time is lacking. It is probable that team members would need to be seconded for a period of time in order to do this effectively. Even so, much progress has been made in many Berkshire schools and the team has certainly played a large part in this. A great many of Berkshire teachers have been involved in at least one of the team's courses and over half of the secondary schools have had some involvement.

The team's expertise has also been called upon in the running of courses and workshops for the Berkshire T.R.I.S.T. programme which some participating schools have used to further their PSE programmes. This expertise and experience is also available for G.R.I.S.T. (Grant-related in-service training). The effect of moving to the "problem-solving" model of curriculum change has thus been to create a team capable of helping teachers to analyse their own needs and to produce their own materials from a variety of resources. It is thus able to provide support for a variety of models of in-service training, including school-based work.

SANDHURST SCHOOL: THE INTRODUCTION OF TUTORIAL WORK

Introduction

From 1979, with the publication of the first of the

Managing Change: Two Case Studies

Active Tutorial Work books and the subsequent training programmes, a great deal of interest has been taken in the question about what the tutor should do with his group in tutorial time. Tutorial work can be a crucial part of the Personal and Social Education programme of the school; equally it can be time wasted. A great deal of heated discussion has been generated among staff in schools and colleges as to how this time should be used, and it is a matter for each school to settle in the best interests of its pupils. The following case study is designed to show the stages one school went through in implementing a tutorial programme and to suggest some strategies for the management of change which arise from them.

Sandhurst School

Sandhurst School is a co-educational comprehensive school on the Berkshire/Surrey border. There is a stable roll of about 1100, with a 6 form entry, and the school has a Sixth Form containing students of all abilities. The pupils' backgrounds are very mixed. The catchment area contains middle class housing estates, local authority housing estates, a re-housed gypsy population and children of soldiers at the Royal Military Academy. New housing estates are spring up around the school and these seem certain to maintain rolls in the near future.

The pastoral organisation is through a House system. There are four Houses, each contain between 250-300 pupils divided up into 12 tutor groups (2 in each year). It is policy for the tutor to start with his/her tutor group in the first year and remain with them until the end of the fifth year. The sixth form tutors rotate, usually every two years. The tutor is the main link with the home; each tutor is expected to see the parents of each pupil at least twice per year, to discuss the twice-yearly assessments. Many of them do so more often - informal contacts are encouraged and there are other evenings in the school calendar which are designated for tutors who wish to see parents, or who may receive a request for an interview from parents.

Tutorial Work

Until 1983 tutorial time consisted of the last quarter of an hour of each day, 3.45-4.00 p.m. One

Managing Change: Two Case Studies

tutorial time was used for House assembly. The others were used in a variety of ways - discussions, individual counselling, administration and waiting to go home - all happening during this time! It was generally felt to be too short to do any tutorial work which was really worthwhile; also both tutors and pupils were too tired to embark on anything meaningful. Even so, some attempts were made after one Head of House, Carole Chevally, became involved in Active Tutorial Work and became a trainer in Berkshire. It was felt that the scheme would provide a worthwhile programme, if tutorial time could be re-allocated into larger blocks. A rationale for a scheme had already been developed, therefore, when Terry Enright was appointed Headmaster in 1982. Soon after his appointment a residential staff conference, attended by over half the staff, allowed for group discussions which led to a package of changes. Tutorial time was re-allocated to last from 1.45-2.20 p.m. on Tuesdays, Wednesdays and Thursdays, the day was split - 6/2 with six periods before lunch and two after tutorial time, contact time was reduced from 40 minutes per lesson to 35 minutes, and the school day started and finished earlier. On Mondays and Fridays there were to be no tutor periods, so school was to finish earlier. One of the tutorial times would be used for an assembly, so effectively, the period for tutorial work became 2 x 30 minutes, allowing for registration. As a result of this package, time was created for tutorial time and many staff were won over by their support for the other changes.

Planning the programme

The Head gave Carole Chevally and Iris Morrish, the Deputy Head, the rest of the academic year to ensure that a tutorial programme was planned. It was to involve all pupils in all years. The Deputy and the Heads of House thus began the task of preparing a detailed syllabus and lesson plans for years 1-5 based on the Lancashire scheme with additions and deletions. Staff were consulted as to whether they wanted such detailed schemes and the majority said they did. It was stressed, however, that these plans were not compulsory and they were not to be used slavishly; they were designed to save extra work for staff who wished to save time. In the summer of 1983 metings of all tutors were held in year groups and they were given the syllabus (including aims and objectives) for the year and detailed lesson plans. Each Head of House co-ordinated a year group; this was useful for breaking across House barriers. From September 1984 year co-ordinators (unpaid) were appointed to take on the role of guiding each year team, an essential step to ensure uniformity within a House system. All materials and appendices required by the tutors were printed and filed centrally in the library for easy access.

As might be expected in all schools, some staff were not easily won over. There was some criticism of the plan to introduce tutorial work in September 1983 and certainly a minority of staff felt then; and still do, that "academic" work, is a priority and tutorial work a waste of time. However, strong support from senior management helped to ensure that a good start was made. The Head, Deputy Heads, and Heads of House and their deputies were all available and willing to participate in the tutorial work and were widely used. Some devised a regular programme of visits to tutor groups planned in advanced and printed at the beginning of term. They were also available to take small groups of pupils who may be requiring special attention or help.

This support from senior management did much to encourage commitment from many of the staff who were, in any case, involved in the original discussions. The children were already used to "tutor time" but there was resistance from some pupils in the senior school who, despite explanations to the contrary, regarded the tutorial programme as an imposition, with little reference to them. They accepted more readily the study skills and careers work but saw the personal relationship side of the course as "a waste of time". New pupils accepted tutor time as a matter of course, an acceptance which has moved gradually through the school. Parents and governors were notified of the changes as part of the new package of changes and an evening was arranged with the Parent Teacher Association to show parents what happens in tutor time.

Implementation

The tutorial work scheme began in the autumn term of 1983. It was soon apparent, as had been anticipated, that some staff did not feel confident with some of the material or the approaches involving group work and role play. Training sessions and workshops were organised both inside and outside school, sometimes

Managing Change: Two Case Studies

during the lunch hour, at other times during time which had traditionally been set aside for meetings, and sometimes in extra voluntary sessions. Some meetings for year tutors have been timetabled by freeing them while year assemblies are being held by senior staff.

By the following year several advantages and disadvantages could be identified:

1. Pupils in years 1 and 2 accepted the programme and enjoyed aspects of the work. They participated in sessions and could articulate, in most case, what they were getting from the tutorial programme.

2. Tutors and other teaching staff noted the establishment of a sense of group identity and support in some tutor groups.

3. Some tutors who were unconvinced at the inception of the course became "converts" as vociferous in their support as they were in their original condemnation. This has had positive effects on some less committed staff.

4. It was established that every group was "working" in tutorial time - it was just not a time for pupils to sit in idle gossip and staff to prepare for the next lesson. Each group had a progress chart showing the year's programme and items covered could be ticked off. This was also invaluable in case of staff absence, when by checking the progress chart, it was easy to provide work for the tutorial lessons.

5. The longer tutorial period made administration easier. There were times when it was necessary to give out newsletters, invitations, etc. and discussion of these was all part of the programme. Some tutors put their groups together for exchange of information, TV programmes, visits from members of staff or guests from outside school, and preparation of assemblies, when it seemed appropriate.

6. There was a definite "spin off" in that the methods used in tutorial work carried over into other subject lessons.

There were, however, some potential drawbacks:

1. Resistances from <u>some</u> pupils, especially older

137

ones.

2. Staff training needs to be carefully planned.

3. Some of the material prepared was not "successful" in its original form. There was a constant process of reviewing, re-assessing and rejecting some material. Successful activities were also added to the course where relevant.

4. It meant an extra teaching load for tutors. However well prepared the lesson plan and notes were, the tutor still had to take the tutorial session and participate with the group and on two days a week that effectively meant a 9 period day. Some tutors commented on this, even where they were committed to a tutorial programme.

5. Probably the greatest disadvantage was that a tutor group, as with a teaching group in any subject, that had a tutor who was uninterested in tutorial work, had a less interesting and rewarding experience that a group whose tutor agreed with the aims of the course and did his best to work with his group, pursuing their personal and social development.

Evaluation of the scheme was done largely through staff discussion and organised feedback from pupils, both written and oral. Further evaluation and review is continuing and there is a firm commitment to involve the pupils themselves in this. A member of staff has been given a scale post to co-ordinate the programme and evaluation is part of the brief.

Sandhurst School was thus able to move from unpromising beginnings to a situation where tutorial work is now being done throughout the school. In retrospect, the feeling is that it was perhaps very rash to take on the job of starting the scheme in all years at the same time as it meant an enormous amount of work and did lead to some resistance. It may have been better to introduce the scheme in the First Year, but it would then have taken years to work through. It is probable that some kind of compromise is possible. However, tutorial work is now firmly established and continuing, although this was inevitably affected by industrial action in 1985/86.

The management of change

Managing Change: Two Case Studies

The Sandhurst case study highlights some of the strategies which can be used in managing change in this area. The management of change in pastoral care has not always been easy or successful and many schools have had great difficulty in implementing Active Tutorial Work. Too little thought and planning led in many cases to outright hostility. Almost inevitably in pastoral care many teachers see whatever is asked of them as an "extra" to their "real" job of teaching; this factor has to be taken into account when framing policies. The following points are worth considering when planning change with regard to pastoral care:

1. Sort out an adequate rationale for the change. It is necessary to be prepared to argue a case, to convince and to persuade teachers, parents, governors and children.

2. It is useful to have more than one strategy; if the argument is either/or it is likely that one of them may be accepted.

3. It is helpful to have the support of the headteacher, <u>active</u> if possible. Often headteachers are perceived to be unsupportive when what has really happened is that they have not been adequately persuaded of the rationale. This is where clarity of aim is so useful.

4. It is important to look for support in the school. If the innovation is really worth pursuing, some staff are bound to be supportive, if the rationale and planning are right. The problem is that those who criticise, often in a minority, sound the loudest; the important thing is to use the support. It is often useful to form a work group to pilot a project, keeping the objectives simple.

5. It is often possible to obtain support from outside the school, from Advisers, County Support Groups, local NAPCE meetings, other teachers who have carried out similar work in other schools. An outside change agent can take much of the possible hostility away from the innovator in school and can given status to the innovation. It is as well to remember here that staff will soon become discontented with the "hero innovator" who gets too far out in front; he/she will find that it will all be left to him or her!

6. <u>Time</u> is essential, particularly for a curriculum initiative. Time is needed both for the planning and the teaching; a curriculum initiative needs timetabling and resourcing properly. The pastoral head will need to push for these, therefore.

7. Pastoral heads will need to seek means to build teams as no-one can do all the work alone. Effective delegation is necessary. At the same time, however, the pastoral head must be prepared to produce resources and organise their retrieval, as well as helping out at the "chalkface" - in the classroom.

8. With any curriculum initiative, such as tutorial work, it is essential to ensure that the topic is not being covered already. It is, therefore, necessary to establish what is being done and to co-ordinate the programme.

9. An adequate in-service training policy is essential if the potential problems of staff lack of confidence, opposition, apathy etc. are to be overcome. Staff should not be blamed for not accepting methods which they find threatening. The new in-service training arrangements after March 1987 require local authorities to consult schools about their INSET needs. It is important that pastoral heads should lobby hard in their authorities to ensure that training for pastoral care is adequately funded.

10. Evaluation of all courses is necessary, as it ought to be in any part of the curriculum. Modifications and improvements can follow most successfully if the pupils are involved in the evaluation.

11. Communication is an essential ingredient of all aspects of pastoral care. The circulation of the findings of the evaluation will ensure that the support group keeps going and may attract more support.

Innovation in pastoral care is rarely easy, particularly at a time of contraction and decreasing morale. It is, however, possible with careful planning and persistence backed by a sound rationale.
If the guidance is to become a central part of the curriculum for all pupils its aims, activities and methods will need to be understood and to

permeate the whole school curriculum. The introduction of a tutorial work scheme is one strategy for starting to bring this about. It will certainly help to ensure that the "pastoral dimension" of Personal and Social Education is strong.

CHAPTER 7

A NEW CURRICULUM?

> "Higher standards in school education will also reinforce those Government policies outside education which are designed to strengthen the economic and social fabric of our society. More rapid technological change in an increasingly competitive world places a premium on enterprise, personal versatility, and national cohesion".
> DES (1985).

Our schools are expected to achieve a great deal for a great many people, and in recent years, much attention has been devoted to examine how well equipped they are to fulfil these expectations. Handy (1984) adopts a rather different but fruitful examination of schools as organisations. In considering the pupils he asks "are they workers, clients or products?" Workers are members of the organisation who co-operate in a joint endeavour; clients are the beneficiaries of the organisation who are served by the endeavour, whilst products are the output of the organisation, which are shaped and developed by it." He concludes that, from age 11 to 16, pupils are in "a production system gone frantic", and describes schools as "designed to produce confused identities, anomie and powerlessness." However, he does add that this situation is logical if the pupil is seen as a product in the making, moving from specialist process to specialist process in batches of differing quality, graded and inspected individually.
In drawing parallels between schools and business organisations, Handy adds that the pupil can be seen as the customer and "that the pastoral organisation that grew up in comprehensive schools was an intuitive response to this, an internal agency to

A New Curriculum?

make sure that each child got the best mix available out of the product range on offer". However, this "internal marketing system" is not the dominant one in most schools, rather the "production system" predominates. Recent Government initiatives such as TVEI can be seen as attempts to improve the efficiency of the "production system" as well as altering its direction.

Having an efficient "production system" is at the expense of many of the "progressive" ideas associated with educational development in the 1950s and 1960s. Hughes (1985) draws attention to the new approach to conservative educational policy makers encouraging the "re-emergence of both elitist notions and of highly simplistic views about the preferability of traditional methods, of hard work and high standards and of 'tough minded' attitudes to the problems and needs of young people. In these circumstances, the growing conflict between counselling and establishment values might seem inevitable." This change in philosophy has been accompanied by cutbacks in funding which has led to many school counsellor posts disappearing. However, despite this, there has also been a growth in counselling within schools with the development of pastoral care systems. Such systems may, in Hughes's words, "dilute or distort counselling values" which in the long run could be more dangerous than open opposition to these values.

Hargreaves (1982) also expresses concern about the nature of much pastoral care. He describes the division of pupils into "tutor" groups, "house" groups or "year" groups as often little more than an administrative convenience having little significance upon their lives. The mixture of disciplinary and caring functions is also a hazardous combination. Quicke (1985) advocates that pastoral care should not be too strongly linked to personal and social education for the same reason. Pastoral teachers "in the final analysis, whatever their ideals, their aims in practice are about getting pupils to obey authority or conform to social norms". He adds that pastoral and social education is "not about adjustment to the status quo, but more about understanding the nature of the status quo and alternative views about social action in relation to the existing order".

In discussing guidance, counselling or personal and social education, ultimately the issue of freedom arises. These activities are concerned with allowing pupils to explore their "objective" selves within an educational system that lays a heavy emphasis on the

A New Curriculum?

"intellectual-cognitive". (Hargreaves, 1982). Potentially, they emphasise the uniqueness of the individual, the right to be listened to and to be valued, the opportunity to relate to other pupils and teachers in a direct and honest manner and the chance to make personally appropriate choices. Such an experience is liberating, but is sadly lacking in so many aspects of their lives. The "hidden curriculum" so graphically described by Hargreaves (1982) results in fear, and teaches pupils that learning can only occur in schools. This means that the present secondary school system "largely through the hidden curriculum, exerts on many pupils, particularly but by no means exclusively from the working class, a destruction of their dignity which is so massive and pervasive that few subsequently recover from it". The inherent tension between the true aims of guidance and counselling and the net result of schooling is clearly apparent.

Many of the arguments for expanding vocational education in schools have centred around its relevance and acceptability to young people. In effect, it seems to offer them what they want; a training, a useful education, something interesting, and with a purpose to it. Such a view can be too easily accepted, and masks some essential questions. For instance, Dewey (1916) points out that "to split the system and give to others, less fortunately situated an education conceived mainly as specific trade preparation, is to treat the schools as an agency for transferring the older division of labour and leisure, culture and service, mind and body, directed and directive class, into a society nominally democratic". The Thatcher government, deeply unhappy with schools "unsympathetic to industry", has used the MSC through TVEI, to direct the curriculum in such a way as to ensure that a future labour force is educated in the virtues of enterprise, thr free market and profit.

The quotation at the start of this chapter, from "Better Schools" DES (1985) exemplifies the Thatcher government's aims for education. For "national cohesion", read compliant youngsters who don't riot in the streets, for "personal versatility" read a willingness to enter a youth training scheme, or be unemployed or accept a low paid and boring job, and for "enterprise", read an unquestioning support for capitalism and its values. For the last ten years, there has been a growing attempt to destroy the achievements of progressive education (Hughes, 1985) and alternatives to the "hard headed" functionalism

A New Curriculum?

of Thatcherism have tended to be obscured in the welter pronouncements from the DES and MSC.

However, there are a number of interesting and viable alternative ways of educating for the future, and these alternatives incorporate many of the principles of guidance and counselling. Watts (1984) sees changes in the "work scenario" implying major changes within education. Education would become

(1) A broad preparation for life, including social understanding and awareness and social criticism.

(2) A continuous life long process of learning.

(3) Based on open access, widely available in varied forms within which choices can be made.

(4) A catalyst for social mobility throughout life.

(5) A task shared by and sometimes led by non-professional educators.

(6) A decentralised activity with curricula which are negotiated and evaluated locally.

These changes are largely embodied in a "model of helping" proposed by Law in Kushner and Logan (1984). This model is based upon community interaction theories, and "suggest that life planning and life preparing is undertaken in interaction with a range of social encounters with members of the community". By adopting networking techniques, which are based on "seeking a partnership with those other sources of help and influence" the careers educator and counsellor becomes "a bridge standing between the individual and society".

These other influences exist in home, neighbourhood and community and so often have not been allowed to make a positive impact of the workings of the school. Law is suggesting a form of collaborative curriculum development, using for example experience based learning and work experience. He maintains that a diverse network of contacts generates alternatives which help people cope with unpredictability in their lives. It is not enough to rely on the resources of careers teachers and careers officers, for instance, to help young people cope with the difficult transitions they have to make. There are additional resources within the community that could and should be fed into a supportive network. This is a plea against

145

A New Curriculum?

"bureaucratised and protected exclusivism" that all professions can fall into.

White et al (1985) examine current curriculum developments and attempt to integrate these into a model of learning for those aged between 14 and 18. What they describe is a "different model of learning and a different way of organising learning which enables teachers to treat pupils more as individuals. For many of the young people we are talking about, personal development may be a pre-condition to learning. They may have to be nurtured as people before they are motivated to learn. Therefore, the creation of personal tutoring systems, small groups and work/project based learning are basic themes which have the most fundamental implications for timetabling and teaching methods. It would not be enough to teach social and life skills as a 45 minute subject slot or to think that counselling and career guidance could be ´covered´ by having a careers ´specialist´ or by telling the young people that they can come along with their problems to members of staff ´at any time´. What is needed is a systematic building in of tutorials, small group teaching and learning, and project work cutting across normal subject boundaries".

White et al produce a model which represents

(1) Definite topic areas

Creative arts; communication skills; political, legal and economic studies; information technology and technical literacy; design and technology.

(2) Methods and approaches

Experience based teaching; learning from the work place; problem solving and project work; personal and social development; negotiated curriculum and contract learning; guidance and counselling; modular course design and graded assessment; profiling; community involvement; using residential experience.

(3) Subsuming principles

Multi-cultural education; equal opportunities; pre-vocational.

The model lays particular emphasis on the methods and approaches, in other words the process. This process involves some radical changes in schooling, laying emphasis on the individuality of the pupil,

A New Curriculum?

co-operation between pupils and teachers and increased links with the community. The topic areas cut across traditional subject areas, making clear links with the "pastoral" curriculum. The subsuming principles have been widely accepted, within education and by the MSC, but need to be actively put into operation and not just paid lipservice.

Such changes will make demands upon schools and the curriculum leading to the following developments.

(a) Participation by teachers and pupils in course planning.

(b) Interdisciplinary team teaching.

(c) Block timetabling.

(d) Experience in work and in the community.

(e) Involvement of the wider community.

(f) Periods of reflective learning.

(g) Group work in a congenial atmosphere.

(h) Implementing tutorial systems.

(i) Teaching groups of less than twelve.

In the current climate it is unlikely that the last development will come about, although most of the other ideas are to be seen in some way in many schools.

David Hargreaves (1982) pointed out:

> "The comprehensive school had a difficult birth. It was always an unwanted child for some, who impatiently awaited an opportunity to commit a discreet infanticide. For others it was an infant prodigy which needed to be carefully nurtured and to be defended against envious enemies. It survived".

It cannot, however, be assumed that the future is assured. At the time of writing a small group of people - e.g. Scruton, Cox and Marks - are leading an attack on the comprehensive school which is being given the kind of attention and credence far beyond what it deserves. This attack needs to be taken seriously. For Hargreaves:

A New Curriculum?

> "A clear and assured future for the comprehensive school..... can be provided only if we think out an agreed set of goals and purposes for it and take seriously the old questions: what kind of society do we want, and how is the education system going to help us realise such a society".

He suggests that to achieve this there must be:

- no return to the eleven-plus.

- a drive to make the education system more open and just.

- a school curriculum which will endow all pupils with a sense of their own competences and give them a realistic sense of their strengths and weaknesses.

- a strong sense of corporate solidarity.

As he says:

> "we can no longer afford an education system that for too many pupils is an unpleasant induction into the experience of failure and inferiority".

For Hargreaves, a pre-condition for the satisfactory reconstruction or revision of the comprehensive school curriculum is the abolition of all sixteen-plus public examinations. The advent of G.C.S.E. would appear to make this less likely and all schools will have to develop their curricula, and guidance systems, to take account of public examinations for the foreseeable future.

If comprehensive schools are to survive they will need to be "successful" in traditional terms (i.e. in terms of public examinations) as well as in terms of the personal and social development of young people. Bell and Best (1986) suggest that to bring this about

> "the long-term aim for schools should be the total integration of learning support and pastoral support in the context of a whole school policy for curriculum planning".

A school which appears to have made great strides in this direction - Carlton-Bolling School in

A New Curriculum?

Bradford - featured in an article by Jeremy Sutcliffe in the Times Educational Supplement (14.11.1986). Sutcliffe claims that

> "For a tough, inner-city school, with more than half its pupils Asian, and in an area where unemployment and deprivation are rife, it has confounded all expectations. Academic results have risen; discipline has been improved; and attendance at parents´ evenings has doubled: all in four years".

These four years have been those since the appointment of the headmaster, Mervyn Flecknoe. Factors which have helped bring about this situation are:

- a move to a three lesson (ninety minutes per lesson) day. This cuts out time wasted in movement between lessons and minimises potential opportunities for conflict. It also encourages more field-work and less passive learning.

- a reduction in the number of teachers teaching each student by grouping, for example, geography, history and R.E. into humanities, physics, chemistry and biology into science. Sutcliffe claims that these changes "made better relationships possible and increased ties of loyalty between staff and students". Buckley (1980) has pointed out that "teaching and learning represent a form of relationship between teacher and learner..... There must be an effective relationship if there is to be effective learning. The relationship must be right if learning is to happen. There is a social task before there is any change in development. The notion of ´care´ for a teacher is the creation of that relationship from which learning may follow. The teacher who ´cares´ is the one who teaches effectively".

- a movement away from the passive use of worksheets towards more active ways of involving students in their work.

- an extension of the time tutors have

A New Curriculum?

- with their tutor groups, coupled with the development of a record of personal achievement.

- parents evenings, held between 4 p.m. and 7 p.m. at which these records of achievement are discussed. Flecknoe claims that "Parents were genuinely delighted to read about their children and children were equally proud to display their record of achievement. Conversations with tutors were no longer one-sided analyses of ´what was wrong´, but began with mutual understanding of the child and respect for his or her achievements".

- the introduction, for school-leavers, of a Carlton-Bolling graduation certificate, containing a statement about each student´s positive achievements, attendance and punctuality.

- the abolition of corporal punishment. This was replaced by a staged system of suspension.

- an emphasis on equal opportunities. The school handbook sets out a firm policy on racism, a policy which involves appraisal of the content and style of teaching to avoid bias, and attempts are made to improve the self-esteem and working conditions of girls, through, for example, staff appointments and tutorial work.

- greater involvement with the community. There are, for example, 70 adults enrolled for academic and vocational courses in the sixth form.

- involvement of staff at all stages of the change.

Many of the changes have been preceded by research to review the current situation, so that the need for change was backed by real evidence which indicated desirable directions change should take.

The changes in this school came about because of problems specific to that shool, but the philosophy

A New Curriculum?

adopted - equality of worth and a respect for the contributions and abilities of all students - is one that applies for all schools. The school has attempted to combine the pastoral and academic, to adopt a true pastoral curriculum where the personal and social development of pupils is the concern of subject teachers as well as tutors. The school appears to be facing up to a challenge which all schools have to face, with respect to the place of guidance. Joan Sallis (Times Education Supplement, 9.1.1987), talks about the "real enemies" for teachers:

> "low funding and esteem; government control of teaching and ultimately of thinking; a deeply divided system in which some have careers, others work preparation; some have culture and some have competence; some have physics teachers and others have none; some homes fill the gaps and others don't even know there are any gaps".

In this situation, the crucial question is whether "pastoral care", "guidance", "social and life skills" and the like should be allowed to be used to "pastoralise" the young into accepting the unacceptable (Williamson, 1980) or whether they should truly enable the flowering of the talents of all young people, to help them to become "self-empowered" (Hopson and Scally, 1986). Initiatives such as TVEI, C.P.V.E., Y.T.S., The Pastoral Curriculum, etc. will serve little real purpose unless this question is answered in favour of the interests of the young people themselves. It is argued that "pastoralisation" is unacceptable, that "self-empowerment" must be the aim. In the current climate this will not be easy. The situation effects most crucially all comprehensive schools and there is no room for complacency.

If schools were to adopt ideas and philosophy such as those of White, Hargreaves and Flecknoe, there are great opportunities to make secondary schools places that pupils and teachers will enjoy being part of, that will prepare pupils for the challenges of the adult world and that will make our society both more equitable and more humane.

Appendices

Appendix 1.

PASTORAL CURRICULUM (MARLAND)

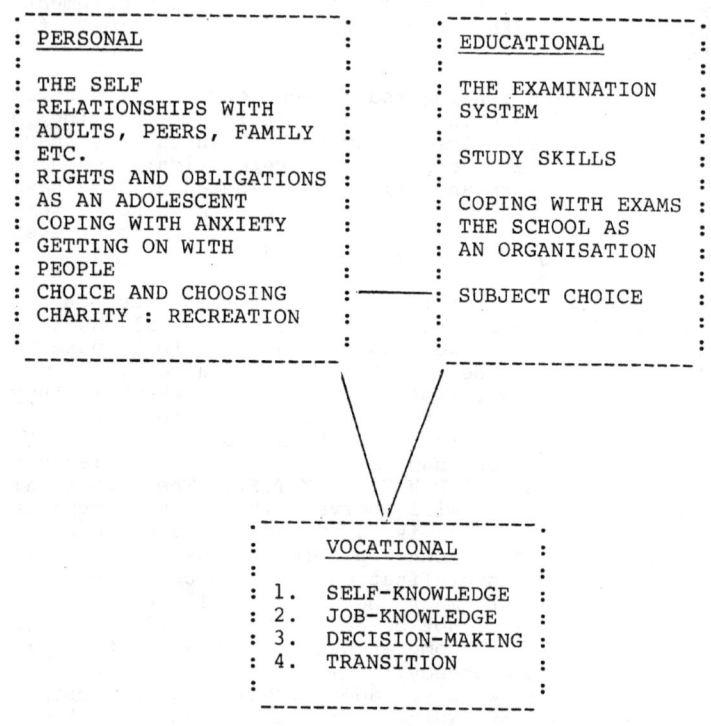

```
: PERSONAL                    :    : EDUCATIONAL        :
:                             :    :                    :
: THE SELF                    :    : THE EXAMINATION    :
: RELATIONSHIPS WITH          :    : SYSTEM             :
: ADULTS, PEERS, FAMILY       :    :                    :
: ETC.                        :    : STUDY SKILLS       :
: RIGHTS AND OBLIGATIONS      :    :                    :
: AS AN ADOLESCENT            :    : COPING WITH EXAMS  :
: COPING WITH ANXIETY         :    : THE SCHOOL AS      :
: GETTING ON WITH             :    : AN ORGANISATION    :
: PEOPLE                      :    :                    :
: CHOICE AND CHOOSING         :————: SUBJECT CHOICE     :
: CHARITY : RECREATION        :    :                    :


                    : VOCATIONAL            :
                    :                       :
                    : 1.  SELF-KNOWLEDGE    :
                    : 2.  JOB-KNOWLEDGE     :
                    : 3.  DECISION-MAKING   :
                    : 4.  TRANSITION        :
```

Appendix 2.

POSSIBLE LOCATIONS FOR THE PASTORAL CURRICULUM

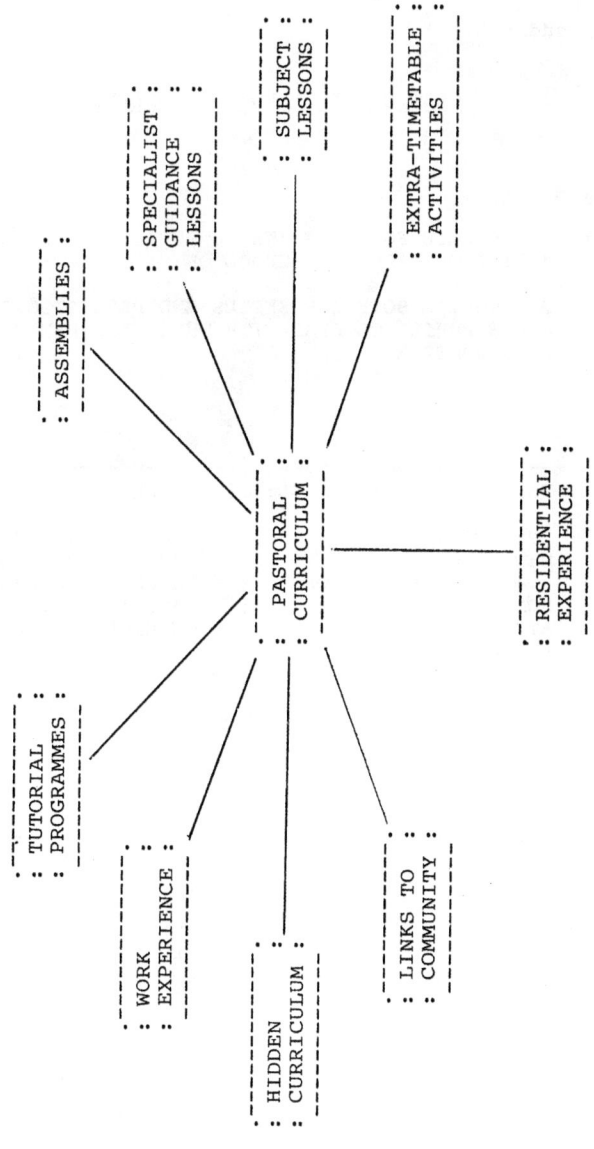

Appendices

Appendix 3.

CRITICAL INCIDENTS (HAMBLIN)

AIMS

(1) TO ISOLATE POINTS AT WHICH PUPILS ARE LIKELY TO AFFILIATE WITH THE SCHOOL OR DISSOCIATE FROM IT.

(2) TO PROVIDE BOTH THE SKILLS AND PERCEPTIONS WHICH ALLOW PUPILS TO DEAL WITH THESE INCIDENTS CONSTRUCTIVELY.

```
.------------------------. .------------------------.
:1. ENTRY INTO THE SCHOOL: :2. THIRD YEAR           :
:                        : :                        :
: - INDUCTION            : : - REASONS FOR CHOICES  :
: - NEW TEACHING         : : - COST OF CHOICES      :
:           SITUATIONS   : : - NATURE OF SUBJECTS   :
: - HOMEWORK             : : - PARENTAL INVOLVEMENT :
: - STUDY SKILLS         : : - CAREERS ADVICE       :
: - EXPANSION OF         : :                        :
:          RELATIONSHIPS : :                        :
:                        : :                        :
 ------------------------   ------------------------
```

```
.------------------------. .------------------------.
:3. 5th YEAR             : :4. 6th/7th YEAR         :
:                        : :                        :
: - PREPARATION FOR EXAMS: : - PREPARATION FOR EXAMS:
: - EXTENDED STUDY SKILLS: : - FOR HIGHER EDUCATION :
: - REVISION TECHNIQUES  : : - NEW STUDY SITUATIONS :
: - ANXIETY/STRESS       : : - CAREERS              :
: - 'A' LEVEL/JOB CHOICE : :                        :
:                        : :                        :
 ------------------------   ------------------------
```

REFERENCES AND FURTHER READING

Active Tutorial Work, Book 5, (1981) B. Blackwell, Oxford
Active Tutorial Work 16-19 (1983) B. Blackwell, Oxford
Avent, C. (1985) Practical Approaches to Careers Education, Hobsons, Cambridge
Ball, Ben (1984) Careers Counselling in Practice, Falmer, Lewes
Banks, Olive (1977) The Sociology of Education, Batsford, London
Baron, S. et al (1981) Unpopular Education, Hutchinson, London
Barry, R. and Wolfe, B. (1962) "Epitaph for Vocational Guidance", Columbia University, U.S.A.
Bates, I. (1983) Participatory teaching methods in theory and in practice - the Schools Council "Careers" Project in School, BJGC, Vol. 11, No. 2
Bates, I. et al (1984)
Bates, I., Clarke, J., Cohen, P., Finn, D., Moore. R. and Willis, P. (1984) Schooling for the Dole? Macmillan, London
Bazalgette, J. (1983) Taking Up The Pupil Role in Pastoral Care, in Education, Vol. 1, No. 3
Beck, C. (1971) Carlton E. Beck, op.cit. See also by the same author, "Philosophical Guidelines for Counselling" (Dubuque, Iowa, C. Brown, 1971)
Beck, J. (1978) "Social and Political Education" in Cambridge Journal of Education, Vol. 8, No. 2
Bell, P. and Best, R. (1986) Supportive Education, Basil Blackwell, Oxford
Benn, C. and Fairley, J. eds. (1986) Challenging the MSC: on Jobs, Training and Education. Pluto Press, London
Berkshire TVEI (1985) Progress Reports, March and October. Berkshire TVEI Centre, Bracknell
Bernbaum, G. (1979) Schooling in Decline, Macmillan, London
Best, R. et al (1977) Pastoral Care: Concept and Process, in British Journal of Educational Studies, 25(2)
Best, R. et al (1980) Perspectives on Pastoral Care, Heinemann Educ., London
Best, R. et al (1982) Education and Care, Heinemann Educ., London
Best, R. and Ribbins, P. (1983) Rethinking the Pastoral-Academic Split, in Pastoral Care in Education, Vol. 1, No. 1
Best, R. et al (1984) Careers Education and the Welfare Curriculum, in Pastoral Care in

References and Further Reading

Education, Vol. 2, No. 1
Blackburn, K. (1975) The Tutor, Heinemann, London
Blackburn, K. (1980) The Tutor: a developing role, in Best, R. et al Perspectives on Pastoral Care, Heinemann Educ., London
Blackburn, K. (1983) Head of House, Head of Year, Heinemann, London
Bolam, R. and Medlock, P. (1985) Active Tutorial Work, Basil Blackwell, Oxford
Bolger, A.W. ed. (1982) Counselling in Britain, Batsford, London
Bould, J. and Hopson, B. (1983) in Marland, M. (ed.) "Sex Differentiation and Schooling", Heinemann, London
Brandes, D. and Ginnis, P. (1986) A Guide to Student-Centred Learning, Basil Blackwell, Oxford
Brennan, T. (1981) Political Education and Democracy C.U.P.
Brown, H. et al (1985) The Class of 84: A Study of Girls in the First Year of the Youth Training Scheme. The Fawcett Society and the National Joint Committee of Working Women's Organisations, London
Buckley, J. (1980) The Care of Learning: some implications for school organisation, in Best, R. et al, Perspectives on Pastoral Care, Heinemann Educ., London
Bulman, L. (1984) The Relationship between the pastoral curriculum, the academic curriculum and the pastoral programme, in Pastoral Care in Education, Vol. 2, No. 2
Buswell, C. (1986) Employment Processes and Youth Training, in Walker, S. and Barton, L., Youth, Unemployment and Schooling. Open University Press, Milton Keynes
Button, L. (1974) Developmental Group Work with Adolescents. Hodder and Stoughton, London
Button, L. (1980) The Skills of Group Tutoring in Best, R. et al, Perspectives on Pastoral Care, Heinemann Educ., London
Button, L. (1982) Group Tutoring for the Form Teacher. Hodder and Stoughton, London
Button, L. (1983) The Pastoral Curriculum, in Pastoral Care in Education, Vol. 1, No. 2
Central Advisory Council for Education (1959) "Fifteen to Eighteen" (The Crowther Report), HMSO, London
Chitty, C. (1986) TVEI: The MSC's Trojan Horse in Benn, C. and Fairley, J., Challenging the MSC
Clarendon Commission Report (1864) Quoted in Lang, P. (1984) Pastoral Care: Some Reflections on

References and Further Reading

Possible Influences, in *Pastoral Care in Education*, Vol. 2, No. 2

Clarke, E.J. and Willis, P. (1984) in Bates, I., Clarke, J., Cohen, P., Finn, D., Moore, R. and Willis, P. (1984) *Schooling for the Dole?* Macmillan, London

Coleman, J.C. (1979) *The School Years*, Methuen, London

Crewe, I. (1983) Gallup Survey of 1983 General Election, "Guardian", 13.6.83

Crick, B. and Heater, D. (1977) *Essays on Political Education*, Falmer, Lewes

Crick, B. and Lister, I. (1978) in Crick, B. and Porter, A., "Political Education and Political Literacy". Longman, London

Crick, B. and Porter, A. eds. (1978) *Political Education and Political Literacy*. Longman, London

Curriculum Review Unit (1983) "Teaching Political Literacy", Bedford Way Papers

Dale, R. (1985) *Education, Training and Employment*. Pergamon, Oxford

Dale, R. (1986) Examining the Gift-Horse's Teeth: a Tentative Analysis of TVEI in Walker, S. and Barton, L., *Youth, Unemployment and Schooling*. Open University Press, Milton Keynes

Dauncey, G. (1981) "The Unemployment Handbook", N.E.C., Cambridge

Daunt, P. (1975) *Comprehensive Values*, Heinemann Educ., London

David, K. (1983) *Personal and Social Education in Secondary Schools*. Longman, London

Davies, M. (1985) *Escape From Alcatraz* in TVEI Insight, March 1985, MSC

Daws, P. (1977) Are Careers Education Programmes in Secondary Schools a Waste of Time? *British Journal of Guidance and Counselling*, Vol. 5, No. 1

Demaine, J. (1981) "Contemporary Theories in the Sociology of Education", Macmillan, London

Department of Education and Science (1977) in Appendix B, in Crick, B. and Porter, A. "Political Education and Political Literacy". Longman, London

Department of Education and Science (1978) *Curriculum 11-16: Working Papers by Her Majesty's Inspectorate - a contribution to current debate*. HMSO, London

Department of Education and Science (1979) Aspects of Secondary Education in England: a survey by H.M. Inspector of Schools. HMSO, London

Department of Education and Science (1980)

References and Further Reading

Examinations 16-18. HMSO, London

Department of Education and Science (1981) The School Curriculum. HMSO, London

Department of Education and Science (1982) 17+ A New Qualification. HMSO, London

Department of Education and Science (1983) Discussion document. HMSO, London

Department of Education and Science (1985) "Better Schools". HMSO, London

Department of Employment Careers Service Branch (1986) Equal Opportunities for Girls and Boys

Dewey, J. (1916) Democracy and Education. Macmillan, New York

Duffy, M. (1986) What price coherence and ideals? in Times Educational Supplement, 20.6.86.

Eggleston, J. (1977) The Sociology of the School Curriculum. Routledge and Kegan Paul, London

Elliott, J. (1975) in Elliott, J. and Pring, R. eds., Social Education and Social Understanding. University of London Press, London

European Community (1985) Action Handbook - How to implement Gender Equality. EEC, Brussels

Equal Opportunities Commission (1985) The organisation and content of the 5-16 curriculum. EOC, Manchester

Fawcett, B. (1985) What Trace of Careers Education? Longman, London

Fawcett Society (1985) The Class of 84: A Study of Girls in the First Year of the Youth Training Scheme. London

Fiddy, R. and Stronach, I. eds. (1986) TVEI Working Papers 1. Centre for Applied Research in Education, University of East Anglia

Finch, Janet (1984) Education as Social Policy. Longman, London

Finn, D. (1986) YTS: The Jewel in the MSC´s Crown? in Benn, C. and Fairley, J. eds., Challenging the MSC

Further Education Unit Study Group (1979) A Basis for Choice. F.E.U. Publications

Further Education Unit (1980) Response to "Examinations 16-18". F.E.U. Publications

Further Education Unit (1981) "Vocational Preparation". HMSO, London

Further Education Unit (1985) C.P.V.E. in Action

Galton, M. and Moon, R. eds. (1983) Changing Schools ....Changing Curriculum. Harper and Row, London

Gillespie, J. (1981) in Heater, D. and Gillespie, J., "Political Education in Flux". Sage, London

Gleeson, D. (1983) Further Education, Tripartism and the Labour Market, in Gleeson, D. (ed.) Youth

References and Further Reading

Training and the Search for Work. Routledge and Kegan Paul, London
Gleeson, D. (1986) Further Education, Free Enterprise and The Curriculum, in Walker, S. and Barton, L. *Youth, Unemployment and Schooling*. Open University Press, Milton Keynes
Goodhew, E.R. (1981) The Developing Role of the Tutor in the Pastoral Care Context (unpublished M.A. dissertation) Reading University School of Education
Goodhew, E.R. and Johnson, J. (1985) The Berkshire Pastoral Support Team, in *Pastoral Care in Education*, Vol. 3, No. 2
Gothard, W.P. (1985) *Vocational Guidance - Theory and Practice*. Croom Helm, London
Graham, H. (1986) "The Human Face of Psychology". O.U.P., Milton Keynes
Green, A. (1986) The MSC and the Three-Tier Structure of Further Education, in Benn, C. and Fairley, J. *Challenging the MSC*. Pluto Press, London
Hamblin, D. (1978) *The Teacher and Counselling*. Basil Blackwell, Oxford
Hamblin, D. (1978) *The Teacher and Pastoral Care*. Basil Blackwell, Oxford
Hamblin, D. (1986) *A Pastoral Programme*. Basil Blackwell, Oxford
Hamilton, J. (1982) Education, Industry and Society (the Graham Clark lecture), in *Times Educational Supplement*, 23.4.82.
Handy, C. (1984) *Taken for Granted? Understanding Schools as Organisations*. Longman, London
Hanson, L.S. (1974) in Peters and Hansen, "Vocational Guidance and Career Development". McGraw Hill, U.S.A.
Hargreaves, D.H. (1982) *The Challenge for the Comprehensive School*. Routledge and Kegan Paul
Hargreaves, D. Chairman (1984) Improving Secondary Schools - Report of the Committee on the Curriculum and Organisation of Secondary Schools, ILEA
Havelock, R. (1969) *Planning for innovation through dissemination and utilisation of knowledge*. University of Michigan
Heater, D. and Gillespie, J.A. eds. (1981) *Political Education in Flux*. Sage Publications, London
Herbert, C. (1986) The question of equal opportunity, in Fiddy, R. and Stronach, I. eds. (1986) *TVEI Working Papers 1*. Centre for Applied Research in Education, University of East Anglia
H.M.I. (1977) *Curriculum 11-16*, Working Papers. HMSO, London

References and Further Reading

Hibberd, F. (1984) Pastoral Curriculum: can it do the trick? in *Pastoral Care in Education*, Vol. 2, No. 2
Holt, M. (1980) *Schools and Curriculum Change*. McGraw Hill, Maidenhead
Hopson, B. and Hough, P. (1985) *Exercises in Personal and Career Development*. Hopsons, Cambridge
Hopson, B. and Scally, M. (1981) *Lifeskills Teaching*. McGraw Hill, Maidenhead
Hopson, B. and Scally, M. (1981, 1982, 1986) *Lifeskills Teaching Programmes 1, 2, 3*.
Hughes, P.M. (1971) *Guidance and Counselling in Schools*. Pergamon, Oxford
Hughes, P.M. (1985) Guidance and Counselling in Schools. *British Journal of Guidance and Counselling*. Vol. 13, No. 1
Jackson, M. (1986) Make 16 Plus benchmark for pre-vocational standards, in *Times Educational Supplement*, 18.7.86.
Jackson, M. ed. (1986) "Dig deeper" warning to Government on TVEI kitty, in *Times Educational Supplement*, 1.8.86.
Jamieson, I. ed. (1985) *Industry in Education*. Longmans, Harlow
Joint Board for Pre-Vocational Education
  1984 Consultative Document
  1985 CPVE Criteria
  1985 Core Competences Booklet
  CGLI and BTEC Joint Board, London
Kant, L. and Brown, M. (1983) *Jobs for the Girls?* Schools Council, London
Kushner, S. and Logan, T. (1984) *Made in England*. CARE
Lang, P. (1977) Its Easier to Punish us in small groups, in *Times Educational Supplement*, 6.5.77.
Lang, P. (1980) Pastoral Care: problems and choices, in Raybould et al (1980): *Helping the low achiever in the secondary school*: Educational Review occasional publication, No. 7
Lang, P. (1982) *Pastoral Care: concern or contradiction?* M.A. thesis (unpublished), University of Warwick
Lang, P. (1983) How Pupils see it: looking at how pupils perceive pastoral care, in *Pastoral Care in Education*, Vol. 1, No. 3
Lang, P. (1984) *Pastoral Care: Some Reflections on Possible Influences*, in *Pastoral Care in Education*, Vol. 2, No. 2
Lang, P. and Marland, M. eds. (1985) *New Directions in Pastoral Care*. Basil Blackwell, Oxford

References and Further Reading

Law, B. and Watts, A.G. (1977) *Schools, Careers and Community*. CIO Publishing, London

Law, W. (1981) "Careers Education and Curriculum Priorities in Secondary Schools", in *Educational Analysis*, Vol. 3, No. 2, pp.53-64.

Lawton, D. (1980) *The Politics of the School Curriculum*. Routledge and Kegan Paul, London

Lawton, D. (1983) *Curriculum Studies and Educational Planning*. Hodder and Stoughton, London

Lee, R. (1984) *Beyond Coping*. Further Education Unit.

MSC (1975) "Vocational Preparation for Young People". HMSO, London

Manpower Services Commission (1981) A New Training Initiative: a consultative document

Manpower Services Commission (1982) Youth Task Group Report. MSC.

Manpower Services Commission, Youth Training Board (1985) *Ethnic Minorities and the Youth Training Schemes*, February 1985

Marland, M. (1974) *Pastoral Care*. Heinemann Educ., London

Marland, M. (1980) The Pastoral Curriculum, in Best, R. et al, *Perspectives on Pastoral Care*

Marsh, S. (1986) Women and the MSC, in Benn, C. and Fairley, J., *Challenging the MSC*. Pluto Press, London

McGuinness, J.B. (1982) *Planned Pastoral Care*. McGraw Hill, London

McGuire, James and Priestley, Philip (1981) *Life after school*. Pergamon, Oxford

McLaughlin, T.H. (1983) The Pastoral Curriculum: Concept and Principles, in *Educational Analysis*, Vol. 5, No. 3

Mercer, G. (1974) "Are we being fair to political education?" Research in Education, 11, pp.51-65.

Miller, J. (1983) Tutoring. F.E.U.

Moore, R. (1984) in Bates, I., Clarke, J., Cohen, P., Finn, D., Moore, R. and Willis, P. *Schooling for the Dole?* Macmillan, London

National Youth Bureau (1983) *Curriculum Issues: a handbook for Youth Service providers of the Youth Training Scheme*. N.Y.B., Leicester

Grubb Norton, W. and Lazerson, W. (1981) Vocational solutions to youth problems: the persistant frustrations of the American experience, in *Educational Analysis*, Vol. 3, No. 2

O'Keefe, D. ed. (1986) *The Wayward Curriculum*. Social Affairs Unit, London

Parkins, (1986) in O'Keefe, D. ed. *The Wayward Curriculum*. Social Affairs Unit, London

Phares, J.E. (1976) *Locus of Control in Personality*.

References and Further Reading

General Learning Press, New Jersey
Pollert, A. (1986) The MSC and Ethnic Minorities, in Benn, C. and Fairley, J., *Challenging the MSC*. Pluto Press, London
Porter, A. (1982) "Social and Political Education", in *Cambridge Journal of Education*, Vol. 12, No. 1
Porter, A. (1983) *Teaching Political Literacy*. Bedford Way Paper 16
Pring, R. (1984) *Personal and Social Education in the Curriculum*. Hodder and Stoughton, London
Pring, R. (1985) *A Form of Life*, in Times Educational Supplement, 14.6.85.
Pring, R. (1986) Unnecessary Polarisation, in *Times Educational Supplement*, 20.6.86.
Quirke, J. (1985) Charting a course for Personal and Social Education. *Pastoral Care in Education*, Vol. 3, No. 2
Rampton (1981) Rampton Report. HMSO, London
Regan (1986) in O´Keefe, D. ed. (1986) *The Wayward Curriculum*. Social Affairs Unit, London
Rennie, J. et al (1974) *Social Education: an experiment in 4 secondary schools*. Evans/Methuen Educ.
Richardson, J. (1979) Objections to Personal Counselling in Schools. *British Journal of Guidance and Counselling*, Vol. 7, No. 2
Roberts, K. (1977) The Social Conditions, Consequences and Limitations of Careers Guidance. *British Journal of Guidance and Counselling*, Vol. 5, No. 1
Rogers, Bill (1984) *Careers Education and Guidance*. Hobsons, Cambridge
Rogers, C. (1985) Carl Rogers on Personal Power. Constable, London
Ryan, P. (1984) The New Training Initiative after Two Years, in *Lloyds Bank Review*, April 1984
Sallis, J. (1987) Good news, bad news, in *Times Educational Supplement*, 9.1.87.
Sarup, M. (1982) *Education, State and Crisis*. Routledge and Kegan Paul, London
Schools Council (1984) *Political Education*. Schools Council Publication, London
Scrimshaw, P. (1981) *Community Service, S. Ed. and the Curriculum*. Hodder and Stoughton, London
Scruton (1986) in O´Keefe, D. ed. (1986) *The Wayward Curriculum*. Social Affairs Unit, London
Shertzer, B. and Stone, S.C. (1981) *Fundamentals of Guidance*, 4th ed. Houghton Mifflin, Boston
Silver, H. (1983) *Education as History*. Methuen, London
Simon, B. (1984) *Can Schools Learn?*

References and Further Reading

Smith, D. (1973) Distribution Processes and Power Relations in Education Systems, Block 1, "Education, Economy and Politics". Open University Press, Milton Keynes

Sockett (1975) in Elliott, J. and Pring, R. (1975) Social Education and Social Understanding. University of London Press, London

Solomos, J. (1986) The Social and Political Content of Black Youth Unemployment: a Decade of Policy Developments and the Limits of Reform, in Walker, S. and Barton, 1., Youth, Unemployment and Schooling. Open University Press, Milton Keynes

Storer, G. (1986) First Year Report, in Times Educational Supplement, June 1986

Stradling, R. (1977) The Political Awareness of the School Leaver. Hansard Society, London

Stradling, R. and Norton (1983) The Provision of Political Education in Schools: A National Survey. Curriculum Review Unit, Bedford Way Papers, London

Stradling, R. et al (1984) Teaching Controversial Issues. Edward Arnold, London

Super, D. (1981) in Watts, A.G., Super, D. and Kidd, J.M., "Career Development in Britain". Hobsons, London

Sutcliffe, J. (1986) Rise and Shine, in Times Educational Supplement, 14.11.86.

Swann Report (1985) HMSO, London

Tapper, T. and Salter, B. (1978) Education and the Political Order. Macmillan, London

Taylor (1970) in Elliott, J. and Pring, R. (1975) Social Education and Social Understanding. University of London Press, London

TVEI Insight Industry Year, 1986, MSC. April 1986

Varlaam, C. ed. (1984) Rethinking Transition: Educational Innovation and the Transition to Adult Life. Falmer, Lewes

Walker, S. and Barton, L. eds. (1986) Youth, Unemployment and Schooling. Open University Press, Milton Keynes

Wallace, R.G. (1985) Introducing Technical and Vocational Education.

Watkins, C. (1985) Does Pastoral Care = Personal and Social Education? in Pastoral Care in Education, Vol. 3, No. 3

Watts, A.G. (1984) Education, Unemployment and the Future of Work. Open University Press, Milton Keynes

Watts, A.G. (1985) Education and employment: the traditional bonds, in Dale, R., Education,

References and Further Reading

Training and Employment. Pergamon Press, Oxford
Watts, A.G. (1986) The Careers Service and Schools: a changing relationship. *British Journal of Guidance and Counselling*, Vol. 14, No. 2
Watts, A.G. and Herr, E.L. (1976) Careers Education in Britain and the USA: Contrasts and common problems. *British Journal of Guidance and Counselling*, Vol. 4, No. 2
Watts, A.G. and Law, W. (1977) Schools, Careers and Community. CIO Publishing, London
Watts, A.G. and Law, W. (1985) Issues for Careers Education in the Multi-Ethnic classroom, in *Pastoral Care*, Vol. 3, No. 2
Weiner, M. (1981) *English Culture and the Decline of Industrial Spirit*. Cambridge University Press, Cambridge
West, M. and Newton, P. (1983) The Transition from School to Work. Croom Helm, London
White, J. (1982) *The aims of education restated*. Routledge and Kegan Paul, London
White, R., Pring, R. and Brockington, D. (1985) *The 14-18 Curriculum: Integrating CPVE, YTS, TVEI?* Youth Education Service, Bristol
Whitty, G. (1985) *Sociology and School Knowledge*. Methuen, London
Whyld, J. (1983) Sexism and the Secondary Curriculum. Harper Row, London
Whyte, J. (1981) in *Integrating Careers Education*. Dundee College of Education
Whyte, J. ed. et al (1985) *Girl Friendly Schooling*. Methuen, London
Williams, R. (1961) *The Long Revolution*. Chatto and Windus, London
Williams, T. and Williams, N. (1980) *Personal and Social Development in the School Curriculum*. School Council Publications, London
Williamson, D. (1980) "Pastoral Care" or "Pastoralisation"? in Best, R. et al (1980) *Perspectives on Pastoral Care*. Heinemann Educ., London
Wilson (1970) in Elliott, J. and Pring, R. (1975) Social Education and Social Understanding. University of London Press, London

INDEX

A Basis for Choice 60, 62, 71, 76
Active Tutorial Work 28, 35, 45, 89, 120-121, 129, 131, 133, 135, 139
A New Training Initiative 75

Baldwin,J. 28, 29, 129, 130
Baron,S. 7
Barry,R. and Wolf 86-87
Bates,I. et al 4, 90, 103, 104
Benn,C. and Fairley,J. 48, 60, 67, 68
Berkshire Pastoral Support Team 45, 128-132
Berkshire TVEI 69
Best,R. et al 3, 15, 16, 18, 44, 108
Better Schools (White Paper) 3-7, 49, 63, 71, 85, 144
Blackburn,K. 15, 19, 44
Bolam,R. and Medlock,P. 121
Brandes,P. and Ginnis,P. 70
BTEC 57, 74, 75
Bulman,L. 35
Buswell,C. 79
Button,L. 26, 27, 28, 29, 38, 45, 121

Careers Education, 7 21, 27, 29, 34, 55, 57, 85-109
Careers Service 80
Careers Service Branch 96
Carlton-Bolling School 148-50
Chandler, Sir Geoffrey 48
Chevally,C. 135
Chitty,C. 65, 67, 82
City and Guilds 71
Clarendon Commission 19
Clarke,J. 6
Comprehensive Schools 19, 21, 23, 48, 52, 53, 54, 67
Counselling 3, 8-11, 12, 15, 21, 22, 44, 58, 61, 62, 69, 72, 74, 78, 80, 81, 83
CPVE 45, 47, 55, 57, 60, 62, 69, 71-75, 82
CPVE in Action 73
Crick,B. 115, 116
Critical Incidents 23, 24, 154
Crowther Report 51, 52, 56, 60
CSE 52, 62, 71
Curriculum Review Unit 110, 114, 122

Index

Dale,R. 81
Daunt,P. 52, 82
David,K. 8
Davies,M. 66, 70
Daws,P. 91
Demaine,J. 109
Department of Education
    and Science 20, 48
Dewey,J. 5, 126, 144
Disciplinary functions
    14
Duffy,M. 75

Eggleston,J. 2-3, 99
EITB 79
Elementary Schools 20, 51
Elliott,J. 39, 104-5
Enright,T. 135
Equal Opportunities
    69-70, 73-4, 77, 78,
    79, 94-99
Equal Opportunities
    Commission 94-5, 96

Fawcett,B. 106-7
Fawcett Society 80
FEU 10, 60, 62, 74, 80,
    81
Fiddy,R. and Stronach,I.
    66, 69
Finn,D. 76, 78, 79

Galton,M. and Moon,R. 50
GCE 52, 54, 57, 59, 60,
    62, 71
GCSE 45, 59, 62, 71, 73,
    82
Gleeson,D. 57
Goodhew,T. 13
Goodhew,T. and Johnson,J.
    45
Graham Clark Lecture 56
Grammar Schools 19, 44,
    50, 51, 54, 66, 67
Gray,A. 130
Green,A. 57, 82
Green Paper 1977 49
GRIST 66, 133
Group Work 26, 27, 28
Guidance 8-11, 12, 47, 56,
    57, 58, 59, 62, 68, 69,

Guidance cont. 70, 72,
    74, 75, 78, 80, 83,
    140

Hamblin,D. 16, 23, 26,
    29, 42, 88
Hamilton, Sir James 56
Handy,C. 142-143
Hansard Society 115
Hargreaves,D. 2, 17,
    24, 82, 111, 143
    144, 147-8
Hargreaves Report 53
Havelock,R. 129
Head of House 21, 37
Head of Year 14, 15,
    22, 37
Health Education
    Council 28
Herbert,C. 69
Hibberd,F. 39, 40, 41
Hidden Curriculum 17,
    35, 144
Holt,M. 44, 128
Hopson,B. and Scally,M.
    32, 45, 59, 83, 151
Hughes,P. 5, 8, 10,
    143, 144

Ideology 7-8
Income Data Services 79
Industrial Society 79
Industry Year 48

Jamieson,I. 47, 59
JIIG CAL 108
Joint Board 71, 72, 73
joseph, Sir Keith 62

King Edwards School 67

Lang,P. 19, 34, 44
Law,B. 87, 145
Law in Education
    Project 118-119
Lawson,N. 78
Lawton,D. 48, 53
Lee,R. 105, 126
Life Career Rainbow 91
Life Skills 32, 121
Lowe,R. 20

Index

Mansell,J. 73
Marland,M. 12, 13, 15, 22, 26, 29, 34, 42, 44, 152
Marsh,S. 79
McLaughlin,T. 42
Miller,J. 10-11
Mini Enterprise 57
Model of Helping 145-6
Morrish,I. 135
MSC 1, 64, 65, 70, 71, 75, 76, 77, 79, 81, 85, 92, 144

New Right 112, 125
New Vocationalism 48-9, 50, 56, 57, 58, 59, 60, 63, 68, 82
Norton Grubb,W. and Lazerson,W. 59
Nuffield 129

Pastoral/Academic Split 21, 24, 44
Pastoralization 18
Pastoral Care 3, 13, 15, 16, 18, 19, 20, 24, 34, 36, 37, 38, 40, 41, 42, 43, 44, 45, 46, 52, 68, 143
Pastoral Casework 36, 37, 38, 41, 46
Pastoral Curriculum 12, 22, 23, 26, 29, 34, 35, 36, 37, 38, 40, 41, 42, 43, 44, 45, 46, 52, 68, 113, 152-3
Pastoral Management 37, 46
Pastoral Systems 12, 13, 15, 16, 18, 21, 25, 42, 43, 44, 45
Personal Power 113
Political competence 120, 122
Political Literacy 116
Pollert,A. 78
Porter,R. 111, 123
Pring,R. 43, 83, 120
Private Teaching Agency 78
Product Teaching 18
Profiling 62, 72, 74, 81
Programme for Political Education 112-118
Progressivism 5-6
Public Schools 19, 20, 21, 44

Raikes,R. 20
Rampton Report 99
Red books 53, 82
Richardson,J. 10
Rivendell School 15
Roberts,K. 56, 89, 90, 91
Rogers,B. 86
Rogers,C. 113-114
Role Play 40
Royal Military Academy 134
Ryan,P. 79

Sallis,J. 151
Sadhurst School 133-138
Sarup,M. 5, 8
Schools Council 30, 31, 80, 129
Schools Council Careers Education Project 87, 99-106
Schools Council Humanities Project 104-5, 125
Secondary Modern School 51, 54, 67
Seventeen Plus, a new qualification 71
Sexism 94-95
Shertzer,B. and Stone,S. 9, 113-114
Silver,H. 2, 4
Simon,B. 43
Smith,A. 130
Solomos,J. 78
Storer,G. 74
Stradling,R. 109, 111, 116, 120, 121, 125
Super,D. 89, 91
Swann Report 99, 112

167

Index

The School Curriculum (1981) 45, 53
The Secondary Survey (HMI) 54
Training Standards Advisory Service 79
TRIST 45, 66, 133
Tutor 12-16, 18, 19, 21-23, 26-28, 37, 38, 41, 46, 134
Tutorial Programme 19, 23, 34, 37, 41, 134, 136
TVEI 4, 45, 47, 48, 55, 56, 60, 62, 63-71, 73, 75, 81, 82

Unemployment 91-93, 102

Voting 109

Walker,S. and Barton,L. 60
Wallace,R. 58, 62, 66
Watkins,C. 29, 34-36
Watts,A. 50, 54, 55, 59, 85, 88, 90, 92, 97, 108, 145
West,M. and Newton,P. 96
White,R. et al 68, 114, 118, 146-147
Whitty,G. 110, 112, 115, 118, 125, 127
Whyld,J. 95, 96
Whyte,J. 94, 97
Williams,R. 126-127
Williams,T. and Williams,N. 29, 30
Williamson,D. 17, 20, 43, 44
Work Experience 57, 63, 65, 72, 74

Young,D. 64, 66, 68, 70, 77
Youth Task Group 76, 77
Youth Training Scheme 55, 57, 60, 62, 69, 73, 75-80

For Product Safety Concerns and Information please contact our EU representative GPSR@taylorandfrancis.com
Taylor & Francis Verlag GmbH, Kaufingerstraße 24, 80331 München, Germany

www.ingramcontent.com/pod-product-compliance
Lightning Source LLC
Chambersburg PA
CBHW060348190426
43201CB00043B/1772